Introduction

Chapter 1

    Truth about Mortgage Field Service Work

    Acronyms

Chapter 2

    Independent Contractor vs. Employee

    Contractor Legal Agreement

Chapter 3

    Equipment for MFS Work

Chapter 4

    Company Expectations

Chapter 5

    Building the Business

Chapter 6

    How to Perform MFS Work

Chapter 7

    Control Your Labor-Control Your Life

Chapter 8

    Introduction to Piece Rate

INTRODUCTION

When it comes to your financial future, nobody else cares as much as you do. It is more than just working hard, putting away some cash and "hope" for the best. No longer can we rely on our retirement plans and the government to make sure we have a financial future. Through the years we've learned that it doesn't matter how long you have worked; it's about your ability to make and manage your own money.

As you're probably aware, many people have retired before the normal age of 65 and many have kept working into their 70's and unfortunately later. The difference is how they handle their money.

One of the only ways to get what you want is simply to be your own boss. Owning your own business can be a scary thought but a scarier thought is working as a Greeter at a large retail establishment past the retirement age.

There are literally thousands of ways to make money as business owner. In the *Property Preservation Coach*, we will look at the reasons why property preservation may be a decent option for you at this time.

As you look at this business model, keep in mind that it is what you do with what you make that determines how wealthy you end up. Put another way, it's how you spend, or preferably invest, that determines your wealth and obviously the age at which you can retire.

Brad Sugars of Action Coach teaches that a business is not a good business unless it is, "A commercially, profitable enterprise that can eventually operate without you." The *Property Preservation Coach* will teach you how to create a commercially profitable enterprise. It is up to you to decide when there is enough work to hire staff to run the company so that you as the business owner can do the two most important aspects of operating a company; Finding and Training.

This book is written in manual form. It is intended to help you learn and teach others how to run a Mortgage Field Service Business.

Chapter 1

The Truth about Mortgage Field Services (MFS)

MFS service work has been around as long as banks have been foreclosing on properties. Having an occupant in a property is the best way to preserve a property even if they aren't great tenants. Water flowing through pipes, appliances being utilized, HVAC units preserve better in use rather than sitting still.

MFS came about for one reason; to preserve the asset. The asset comes in the form of property, houses and commercial buildings. In most cases, financial institutions will start the preservation process the moment the foreclosure process starts.

Financial institutions cannot afford to have crews do all of the work on the assets so they hire companies to do MFS work for them. With that said, here are the truths about MFS work:

1. **MFS is a relationship business:** The companies that build the relationships will receive the most work. (See chapter 3) The relationship to most financial institutions has to do with: 1. Completing work on time 2. Proper photos 3. Quality workmanship. The relationship is always in that order.

2. **You will be asked to do favors.** Favors typically have to do with doing work on properties that may not be close to your office or dropping everything you are doing in order to make someone in Cleveland happy for the moment.

3. **Most of the money is made through bidding and volume.** If you are looking to make a lot of revenue, it happens through finding

additional work at each property or doing large volume. (see chapter 3)

4. **You are paid 30-40 days after work is completed and uploaded.** Financial institutions tell you that the 30-40 days are necessary. Banks know how money works so they hold it. Make sure you can survive 2 months without payment.

5. **Everything you do must be documented.** The financial institutions don't have people in the field so they rely heavily on picture documentation. If you don't take pictures and cannot prove the work was completed, you will not be paid for the work.

6. **Some of the companies that give you work will take a percentage of your work.** The large federal institutions like Fannie Mae and Freddie Mac will hire large companies to find people like you to do this type of work. They may receive (example) $50 from Fannie Mae for a grass cut and ask you to pay them 25% of that money so you may only receive $38.50 for the grass cut.

7. **Financial institutions don't care about you or your schedule.** The financial institutions don't care about your weekend, holidays, birth of your child, natural disasters when it comes to their schedule. If the work order states 72 hours, they mean 72 hours to have it uploaded into their system. If you are late, they don't pay you and you are still required by their contract to get it to them.

8. **You will not always be treated well.** Most of the financial institutions have strict guidelines when it comes to timing. The

banks simply want the work done on time with proper photos. If this does not happen, the banks may not pay you, assign the work to another vendor or give you less work from that day forward. You may get yelled at, nasty emails, etc. Don't take it personal as the person on the other end does not.

9. **Some of the work you will do requires a licensed contractor.** If you are looking for some higher paying jobs, you will be asked to bid large items such as roof repair, mold remediation, meth remediation, landscaping, kitchen remodel, change out carpet, etc. In many states, counties, provinces, countries, licensed contractors are required to complete these types of jobs.

It may come across as a negative industry. Don't allow the negative aspects to scare you. The fact of the matter is this business can bring in a lot of revenue and more importantly profit. There are small companies that bill millions in services per year. This business does not require anyone to market in order to bring in business. Once the relationship is built, the work will come. It is simply the responsibility of the owner to find more work and keep training the staff. What a great concept!

Terms (Acronyms)
Listed below acronyms used frequently in the MFS industry:

IBPO - Independent Broker Price Opinion (most often referred to as BPO)
ICC - In Conveyance Condition: Means the property is ready to be turned over to the bank. This usually occurs after foreclosure is complete.
MFSC - Mortgage Field Service Company
PBs - Personal Belongings: Personal property of the current or past tenant/owner
PP - Personal Property
PPR - Property Protection and Preservation

UI - United Inch (adding the dimensions across the top and down one side of an opening together)

CFK - Cash for Keys. Many times the financial institutions pay the tenants cash for leaving the premises so the property can convey back to the banks.

QC- Quality Checks

BATF- Bid After The Fact. Sometimes during a routine work order, more damage is found. Example: During a walk through it was discovered that the roof has started to leak into the home thus causing more damage. The roof would need to be tarped until a full bid could be completed.

Trash Out: Cleaning out all the debris left over from the tenant.

Lock Change: Changing out locks to entrances and secure the property.

REO: Real Estate Owned. Banks own the property.

Chapter 2

Employee vs. Independent Contractor

Independent contractors and employees are not the same, and it's important to understand the difference. Knowing this distinction will help you determine what your first hiring move will be and affect how you withhold a variety of taxes and avoid costly legal consequences.

What's the Difference?

An Independent Contractor:
- Operates under a business name
- Has his/her own employees
- Maintains a separate business checking account
- Advertises his/her business' services
- Invoices for work completed
- Has more than one client
- Has own tools and sets own hours
- Keeps business records

An Employee:
- Performs duties dictated or controlled by others
- Is given training for work to be done
- Works for only one employer

Many small businesses rely on independent contractors for their staffing needs. There are many benefits to using contractors over hiring employees:
- Savings in labor costs
- Reduced liability
- Flexibility in hiring and firing

Why Does It Matter?

Misclassification of an individual as an independent contractor may have a number of costly legal consequences.

If your independent contractor is discovered to meet the legal definition of an employee, you may be required to:
- Reimburse them for wages you should've paid them under the Fair Labor Standards Act, including overtime and minimum wage
- Pay back taxes and penalties for federal and state income taxes, Social Security, Medicare and unemployment
- Pay any misclassified injured employees workers' compensation benefits
- Provide employee benefits, including health insurance, retirement, etc.

Tax Requirements

Visit the IRS Independent Contractor or Employee guide to learn about the tax implications of either scenario, download and fill out a form to have the IRS officially determine your workers' status, and find other related resources.

Employment Information

There is no single test for determining if an individual is an independent contractor or an employee under the Fair Labor Standards Act. However, the following guidelines should be taken into account:

- The extent to which the services rendered are an integral part of the principal's business
- The permanency of the relationship
- The amount of the alleged contractor's investment in facilities and equipment

- The nature and degree of control by the principal
- The alleged contractor's opportunities for profit and loss
- The amount of initiative, judgment, or foresight in open market competition with others that is required for the success of the claimed independent contractor
- The degree of independent business organization and operation
- Whether a person is an independent contractor or an employee generally depends on the amount of control exercised by the employer over the work being done. Read Equal Employment Opportunity Laws - Who's Covered? For more information on how to determine whether a person is an independent contractor or an employee, and which are covered under federal laws.

The reasons many MFS companies use independent contractors is because they have their own trucks and their own equipment. It is still an option to hire an employee and then lease their equipment from them as a small percentage of the job.

Contractor Legal Agreement:

The following is copy of suggested Contractor Agreement. The agreement is merely a protection to the owner. Please be advised that as an owner, you should have this document reviewed by your attorney and this agreement in no way constitutes an official contract.

YOUR COMPANY = Your company

Contractor Service Agreement

THIS AGREEMENT entered into and by and between YOUR COMPANY of (PLEASE ENTER YOUR DBA NAME), hereinafter "YOUR COMPANY", located at (PLEASE ENTER YOUR ADDRESS) and _____ (Contractor Name & Company Name) located at_____ (Contractors Address), hereinafter referred to as "Contractor", is made as follows:

Whereas, YOUR COMPANY desires to have property preservation services performed with respect to certain properties located in the state(s) of (_____).

Whereas, Contractor agrees to perform such services under the terms and conditions stated herein and Whereas YOUR COMPANY is in the business of providing property preservation services for its clients. Now therefore, in consideration of the payment of certain fees and the receipt of work the parties mutually agree to the following:

DUTIES: Contractor shall perform preservation services as ordered by YOUR COMPANY for YOUR COMPANY's clients. YOUR COMPANY shall provide Contractor with specific tasks that the Contractor is to perform hereunder, and the dates by which such tasks are to be completed. All work order results shall be due in accordance with dates provided on forms by YOUR COMPANY clients. Contractor shall perform all services promptly and diligently in a workman like manner within the time requested. All services will be performed in accordance with YOUR COMPANY present and future service standards, YOUR COMPANY Property Preservation and REO Training Manual and as otherwise required by YOUR COMPANY clients, HUD, FHA, VHA and other relevant governmental and private entities. YOUR COMPANY Property Protection and Preservation Services Training Manual is defined as any document, paper or electronic, which delineates procedures and requirements relative to the performance of property preservation and REO services and the standards as required by either YOUR COMPANY clients, HUD, FHA, VHA and other relevant governmental and/or private entities. Contractor compliance regarding documentation, evidentiary, and time of performance requirements is a material requirement of the Agreement. Contractor understands that time is of the essence in providing YOUR COMPANY with the information, reports, services, invoices, photographs and other services ordered by YOUR COMPANY pursuant to this Agreement. Contractor further understands and acknowledges that YOUR COMPANY may suffer significant damages in the event Contractor does not perform its duties hereunder in a timely and quality manner as requested and ordered by YOUR COMPANY clients. In the event Contractor fails to complete any task assigned pursuant to this Agreement, YOUR COMPANY may at its sole discretion 1) recover its damages from Contractor by offsetting such sums from future payments for work performed by Contractor prior to or subsequent to Contractor's breached work assignment and 2) engage another qualified party to complete Contractor's property preservation or REO assignment. Damages are such sums as may be withheld from YOUR COMPANY by its clients or which a YOUR COMPANY client requests and receives reimbursement from YOUR COMPANY, ("Charge backs") and/or any profit that YOUR COMPANY was entitled to receive if the Contractor performed the work in accordance with this Agreement Damages may be offset by YOUR COMPANY in the event that the Contractor breaches this Agreement, fails to complete work when due, fails to submit complete documentation supporting work completed in a timely manner and or fails to provide invoices or photographs evidencing work in a timely manner. If YOUR COMPANY engages a third party to complete Contractor's uncompleted property preservation service(s), YOUR COMPANY may withhold and offset from Contractor's future payments, the funds paid to said third party and any profit due to YOUR COMPANY from client which is withheld by client due to delay of completion of service.

WORK ASSIGNMENTS: The parties agree that each job contracted and assigned to Contractor shall be on a job-by-job basis and that this Agreement shall govern all transactions between the parties. YOUR COMPANY reserves the right to reassign work at its sole discretion.

INDEPENDENT CONTRACTOR: Contractor acknowledges that it is an independent Contractor and not an employee of YOUR COMPANY. Contractor shall be solely responsible for all federal, state and local income taxes, unemployment taxes, social security taxes and contributions of any kind, workers compensation insurance, workers compensation premiums and any and all other forms of insurance and/or taxes requited to provide the services outlined in this Agreement. Nothing in this Agreement shall be construed to create an employer/employee relationship, joint venture or partnership agreement between the parties hereto. Contractor is solely responsible for the work to be performed and, other than receiving the request and description of work from YOUR COMPANY; YOUR COMPANY does not have control of or direct the work to be done.

INDEMNITY: Contractor agrees to save, defend and indemnify and hold harmless, YOUR COMPANY from and against any and all claims of any kind, whatsoever arising from (i) any act, omission or negligence by Contractor, Contractor's agents, employee's, representatives, subcontractors and any and all others acting upon Contractor's behalf, or (ii) any accident injury or damage caused to any person or entity, or to the property of any person or entity, where such accident, damage or injury resulted or is claimed to have resulted from any act, omission or negligence on Contractor's part, or (iii) failure to adhere to any applicable law, rule or regulation of any governing body having jurisdiction over work performed pursuant hereto or (iv) any act, omission or default under any of Contractor's undertakings in the Agreement. This indemnity and hold harmless Agreement shall include indemnity against all costs, expenses, fines, liabilities and attorney fees from or in connection with any such claims or proceedings brought here on and the defenses thereof.

INSURANCE: Contractor shall purchase and maintain insurance to protect Contractor from claims under the workman's compensation laws, disability benefit laws or other similar employee benefit laws;

from claims for damage because of bodily injury, occupational sickness or death of its employees, and claims insured by usual personal injury liability coverage; from claims for damage because of bodily injury, sickness, death of any person other than Contractor's employees including claims insured by usual bodily injury, personal injury and/or liability coverage; errors and omissions coverage's, and claims for injury to, loss or destruction of tangible property, including loss of use.

Contractor agrees to purchase and keep in full force and effect during the term of this Agreement workers compensation, general liability, errors and omission and automobile insurance. The minimum amount of such insurance shall be in the amount of $1,000,000 general aggregate limit and $1,000,000 per occurrence limit for insurance policy obtained by Contractor pursuant to the Agreement. Contractor agrees to name YOUR COMPANY as an additionally insured on all such policies and to provide an original duly executed certificate evidencing such insurance, in a form acceptable by YOUR COMPANY, within thirty days of the execution of this Agreement and annually as long as Contractor receives work from YOUR COMPANY.

ENVIRONMENTAL COMPLIANCE: Contractor bears the sole responsibility for determination of the manner and nature of the removal of all debris, trash, hazardous materials, personal property and any and all other materials from properties pursuant to property preservation work orders under this Agreement. Contractor shall perform all material removal and disposal in compliance with all applicable laws. Contractor shall remove and dispose of no items of hazardous waste unless said disposal is in compliance with all applicable local, state and federal environmental laws, rules and regulations. Contractor shall abide by all applicable local, municipal, state and federal rules and regulations regarding the disposal of any and all materials of any kind whatsoever from any property which Contractor performs property preservation services.

CONFIDENTIAL INFORMATION: The Contractor shall not, while performing services pursuant to this agreement or otherwise, disclose or use for the benefit of himself or herself or any other person, corporation, partnership, joint venture, association, or other business organization, any of the trade secrets or confidential business information of YOUR COMPANY. For the purpose of this Agreement, "trade secrets" of YOUR COMPANY shall include, but shall not be limited to, any proprietary and technical information of YOUR COMPANY in the nature of sales, pricing methods, operating systems, and associated procedures and systems, parts, information, programs, services, systems, inventions, business techniques and the like developed or employed by YOUR COMPANY. For the purpose of the Agreement, "confidential business information" of YOUR COMPANY shall include any information this is (i) of any value or significance to YOUR COMPANY and (ii) not generally known to the competitors of YOUR COMPANY nor intended by YOUR COMPANY for general dissemination, including but not limited to any and all proprietary and technical information of YOUR COMPANY in the nature of business operations, operating systems, and associated procedures and systems, accounting and financial data, customers lists, current or potential suppliers/vendors, design systems, pricing and discounting practices, YOUR COMPANY market data, sources of supply, special programs relating to sales, project files, prospect reports, training, products and equipment, and information about YOUR COMPANY itself and its executives, officers, directors, and employees. Contractor acknowledges that in the course of its dealings with YOUR COMPANY, Contractor may receive or learn confidential information concerning their parties to whom YOUR COMPANY has an obligation of confidentiality. ("Confidential Information"). The Confidential Information may include but not be limited to personal and/or financial information about individuals who have applied for or purchased financial products or financial services from Clients to YOUR COMPANY. Contractor agrees that it will keep all Confidential Information strictly confidential; that is will not disclose to any third party, either orally or in writing, any Confidential Information without the prior written consent of YOUR COMPANY; and that Contractor will not appropriate any Confidential information to its own use or the use of any third party. Contractor shall use confidential information that is provided by YOUR COMPANY only for the purpose for which it was provided and access to it shall be restricted to individuals who require the information to further that purpose. Contractor agrees to comply and cooperate with any and all additional privacy and/or confidential information policies as promulgated in the future by clients of YOUR COMPANY.

CONTRACTOR PAYMENTS TO THIRD PARTIES: Contractor shall pay any monies owed to its employees, agents, servants and subcontractors, representative, material men, and suppliers with respect to work on any property assigned to Contractor pursuant to this Agreement Contractor shall not permit or cause any lien to be filed on any property by either Contractor or any third party that provides services to Contractor pursuant to this Agreement. Contractor shall be responsible for all costs incurred in connection with the performance of services hereunder and shall bear any loss or damage to materials, vehicles or other articles held or used in connection with said services.

PAYMENT FOR SERVICES AND CHARGEBACK(S): YOUR COMPANY shall pay Contractor for services rendered in connection with work performed for YOUR COMPANY on a net 30-day basis. Payment to Contractor for services rendered to YOUR COMPANY shall be in Accordance with the YOUR COMPANY Pricing Schedule. The Pricing Schedule is hereby incorporated by reference into this agreement. YOUR COMPANY reserves the right to reduce the amount of any invoice submitted by Contractor where and when said invoice fails to comply with YOUR COMPANY billing deadlines or other documentary, evidentiary, customer or other requirements as may be communicated to Contractor through YOUR COMPANY Property Protection and Preservation Services Training Manual or other means. YOUR COMPANY reserves the right to change said pricing structure at any time based on changes from their clients. Contractor specifically grants to YOUR COMPANY a right of offset against balances due to Contractor, regarding work or documentation of work, which is charged back to YOUR COMPANY by YOUR COMPANY clients, Charge backs to Contractor shall be non negotiable and at the sole discretion of YOUR COMPANY.

BREACH: In the event of Contractor's breach of the terms of this Agreement, either in whole or in part, relative to any property preservation work or REO assignment, YOUR COMPANY may, in addition to any remedies provided within this Agreement, arrange for completion of the preservation or REO service(s) and charge Contractor the cost of said service.

COMPLIANCE WITH LAWS, PAYMENT OF TAXES: Contractor warrants that at all times it shall comply with all applicable federal, state, local and other laws and regulations (and as such laws and regulations may have been amended or may be amended from time to time in the future) in performing the Services and its other obligations pursuant to this Agreement.

DISPUTE RESOLUTION: This agreement shall be governed by and construed in accordance with the laws of the State of (____), in (_____) County, without application of its principles of conflict of law. The parties choose the state and federal courts of (_____) County, (____(State)) as the chosen venue of any litigation between the parties related in any way to this Agreement. The prevailing party in any dispute arising out of or related to this Agreement, shall be entitled to recover the costs incurred, which costs shall include reasonable attorney's fees, in any legal proceedings including all mediation, arbitration, administrative, appellate or Bankruptcy proceedings. Contractor hereby knowingly, voluntarily and intentionally waives any and all rights it may have to a trial by jury regarding any and all litigation arising out of this Agreement or any and all transactions contemplated herein or any course of conduct or dealings, statements (either verbal or written) or actions of any party related thereto. Contractor hereby waives any right it may have to seek to consolidate any such litigation with any other litigation in which a jury trial cannot or has not been waived.

TERMINATION: This Agreement may be terminated with or without cause by either party for any reason. Contractor must give thirty days-notice when terminating agreement. Termination of the Agreement by either party shall not release contractor from any responsibility or liability on the part of Contractor that arises prior to termination. Upon termination of this agreement, YOUR COMPANY may withhold any and all funds due to Contractor for services rendered thru the date of termination for a period of 90 days in order to ascertain the applicable offset, if any.

TERM: Unless terminated by the mutual consent of the parties or as otherwise provided for herein, this Agreement shall be binding on the parties from the effective date of this Agreement and shall thereafter be automatically renewed on a year to year basis unless otherwise determined by the parties.

NOTICE: Any notice provided for in this Agreement shall be given by mailing such notice by certified mail to the address stated in the introductory paragraph or a party designates such other address as in writing.

ENTIRE AGREEMENT: This Agreement sets forth the entire understanding of the parties and merges all prior written and oral communications relating thereto. This Agreement may be modified or amended only in a writing signed by a duly authorized representative of each party.

CHANGES AND MODIFICATIONS: This Agreement may be modified or amended only in writing and signed by a duly authorized representative of each party. Section headings are for the convenience of reference only and shall not be construed otherwise.
WAIVER: No failure to exercise, or delay in exercising, on the part of either party, any right, power or privilege hereunder shall operate as a waiver therefore no will any single or partial exercise of any right, power or privilege hereunder preclude the further exercise of the same right or the exercise of any other right hereunder.

SEVERABILITY: If any part of this Agreement is adjudged by a court of competent jurisdiction to be invalid, such judgment shall not affect nullify the remainder of this Agreement, which shall remain in full force and effect.

ASSIGNMENT: Contractor may not assign, transfer or otherwise delegate any of its rights or responsibilities under and pursuant to this Agreement without the prior written consent of YOUR COMPANY. Any attempted assignment shall be null and void.

REQUIRED EQUIPMENT:
Truck
Trailer
Cell Phone
Answering Machine
Laptop Computer

External Hard Drive
Email (ability to email)
Digital Camera
Air Compressor
Gas Generator
Lawn Maintenance Equipment (mower, edger, shovel, rakes)
Drill (cordless)
Ladder (6' for Interior Projects; 20' for outside duties)
Cleaning Supplies
Yard Maintenance Equipment
Screw Drivers
Hammer

IN WITNESS WHEREOF, the parties have caused this Agreement to be executed, after having the opportunity to read the document thoroughly. The parties agree that they are duly authorized by their legal entity to enter into any and all contracts on behalf of the legal entity. You acknowledge your clear intent to be bound to the terms of YOUR COMPANY (Enter DBA) Contractor Service Agreement.

Signed this _____ day of _____, _____

_____
By Contractor

Signed this _____ day of _____, _____

_____
By YOUR COMPANY of (Enter DBA)

Chapter 3

Equipment for MFS Work:

The extent of the basic tool inventory will depend on the personality of each individual crew. If a crew has the ability to use and inventory a large tool set, they should acquire the set. Having the right tools for the right job will save you time. For example, having the right tools for disassembling an outdoor swing set, a dog run, or exercise machine can save you an abundance of time.

- Truck: Make sure it can tow a dump trailer if needed. ½ Ton truck recommended.
- Trailer: Preferably a hydraulic dump trailer. 12-15 yard is preferred.
- Cell Phone:
- Answering Machine: Cell phone answering machine works well. Have to be able to answer banks quickly. Those that respond faster, get more work.
- Laptop Computer: For uploading, emails and bidding.
- External Hard Drive: For saving photos. Must save for 3 years.
- Email (ability to email)
- Digital Camera: Documenting everything. Purchase additional SD cards.
- Air Compressor: For winterizing and cleaning
- Gas Generator: Many homes have no electricity and to power up the compressor if not gas.
- Lawn Maintenance Equipment: (mower, edger, shovel, rakes)
- Ladder (6' for Interior Projects; 20' for outside duties)
- Cleaning Supplies. Rags, broom, dust pan, mop, Windex, all-purpose cleaner, toilet brush, rubber gloves
- Screw Drivers. Regular and Phillips
- Hammer:

- Snow blower or snow shovel.
- Utility knife: Cut out sheetrock and just nice to have around
- Measuring Tape:
- Claw hammer
- 2lb sledge hammer
- Small hand saw
- 24" bolt cutters
- Hack saw with two extra 18-tooth blades
- Basic set of pliers
- 12" channel locks
- One 10" and one 12" aluminum pipe wrench
- Basic set of screw drivers
- Basic set of wrenches
- 4" putty knife
- Utility knife with extra blades
- Pencils or like marking instruments
- Chalk line
- Flat bar
- Medium crow bar
- Two flash lights
- At least one 18 volt driver drill of "name brand" quality
- 18 volt work light
- 6" 18 volt skill saw
- 18 volt saws

Notes:

All of the battery tools should be of the same brand and voltage and the tool set should contain at least one extra 18 volt battery and charger. We use and have specified 18 volt cordless tools. 14 volt tools are cheaper and lighter to work with. The size/quality of these tools is up to you and experience.

Securing the Property

A complete Kwik Set Re-keying kit. This includes:

- Pins 1 through 7
- A tumbler removal tool
- A follower
- A medium sized pocket knife (not a part of a re-key kit).

"The follower is a small round tool that is held tightly against the rear of the tumbler as the tumbler is removed. The purpose of the follower is to secure the top pins in place while the tumbler is being re-keyed."

- A cordless drill/driver (It is preferred to have two drills of the same make and model, with extra batteries and a charger for your work truck)
- A small set of quality/sharp drill bits
- At least one pair of either 10 or 12 inch channel lock pliers
- 12" flat bar – claw hammer
- 24" crowbar
- ½" wood chisel (sharp)
- 1 flashlight
- Small container such as a medium sized pill bottle (used to store extra lock parts that can quickly replace a part that will inevitably become lost during re-keying. It is much easier to pull an extra part out of your emergency bottle than to try to find a very small part which is lost in the debris on the floor)

Trash Out/Initial Clean
- Trailer – 10-16ft with sides
- 2 tarps – one large enough to cover a load to meet state/local codes, and one approximately 6'x10' on which to pile leaves, grass clippings, and limbs on to drag out of the yard
- 30 gal draw-string 1.1ml trash bags – two 55-bag boxes
- 1 yard stick
- 2 leaf rake
- 1 garden rake
- 1 flat point long handled shovel
- 2 straight straw brooms
- 2 sponge mops – with two extra mop heads
- 1 mop bucket
- Vacuum cleaner with four new bags (if vacuuming is required by your customer)
- Gas Generator (if vacuuming is required by your customer) – at least 20-25amp but no larger than can be carried by one man
- Flat surface cleaning solution – at least one gallon bulk with two spray bottles
- Window cleaning solution – at least one gallon bulk with two spray bottles
- Heavy kitchen grease cleaner – at least one gallon bulk with one spray bottle
- Paper towels – at least six normal sized rolls in stock
- Water – at least two six/seven-gallon plastic cans marked "non-potable water – do not drink"
- 1 four-inch putty knife
- 1 scrubbing brush
- 2 toilet brushes

- 1 toilet plunger
- Two inch clear packing tape with roll dispenser – two rolls, one dispenser
- 1 Dusting Webster with extendable handle
- 1 Dusting Webster with short handle
- 60 watt light bulbs – at least a six in a well-protected carton
- Room deodorizer – at least six
- Arm and Hammer baking soda – at least three small boxes for refrigerators, if requested by client
- 20' extension ladder to clean gutters, prune overhanging tree limbs or access the roof
- 6' step ladder for interior cleaning
- Wheelbarrow – (optional)
- Yellow caution tape – one small roll

Lawn Service

- Lawn mower – commercial machine with extra sharp set of blades
- String trimmer – suggest quality brand commercial, straight-shaft machine
- A second string trimmer that will operate interchangeable attachments such as a hard edger, shrub pruner and a back-up string trimmer, is suggested
- Loppers – one pair, commercial grade
- Tree pruner – one long handled telescoping model
- 1 six foot by ten foot tarp
- 1 five gallon gas can
- One gallon can for mixed gas per each small engine machine of different manufacturer
- Two bottles of mixing oil for each machine with different manufacture

Winterization
- Small electric compressor that will achieve 100lb psi
- Basic "hose to house plumbing" connecting parts – Schrader valve to typical hose connection
- 50' – 75' 5/8 inch garden hose, with extra connecting washers
- RV non-toxic pink anti-freeze – three gallons
- "Winterized" stickers per each individual customer's requirements – 2" clear tape to tape down toilet seats and to install required stickers

Exterior Mildew (for Vinyl Siding)
- Two gallon pressure sprayer
- Eight inch acid brush with extendable handle
- Bleach or equivalent mildew wash – one gallon

Boarding
- Plywood and lumber per client/job requirements – normally ¾" exterior plywood and normal 2"x4"s
- Bolts, nuts, washers per client/job requirement – normally 3/8" x 12" carriage bolts – we normally carry 8", 10" and 12".
- 16 inch x 7/16 inch spiral twist drill bit – a 16" bit will be long enough to drill through most wall thicknesses including the plywood on outside and 2"x4"s on inside. We usually carry 2 full sheets of plywood and 3 or 4 2"x4"x8'.

Miscellaneous
- Two quarts Kilz
- One large paint brush

- One medium paint brush
- Flea/Roach foggers – four cans
- Heavy work gloves
- Disposable cleaning gloves
- Dust masks
- Digital camera with date stamp, one per crew/vehicle (get the least expensive model available)
- 3/16" braided nylon rope
- A pump bottle of hand sanitizer
- First Aid Kit

This list of tools does not list a tool each time it is used in a different scope of work. However, all tools required to perform the different types of PPR services are, for the most part, on this list. Individual crews may have different tool preferences and/or requirements; therefore the overall tool inventory may vary. With proper organization, this list of tools and supplies will comfortably fit in a standard full size utility van and tongue box on your trash out trailer.

Chapter 4
Company Expectations

The key attribute of a successful organization is being "results-oriented". A valuable employee or contractor is able to act according to the circumstances, pursue the results, neither postponing the solution of issues nor multiplying bureaucracy.

Other corporate standards should include:
- Professionalism — to possess unique and up-to-date knowledge and have the capability to apply this knowledge; one's own competent vision and opinion; as well as the capability to achieve results.
- Initiative — to make proposals on new projects, optimize functions and business processes; show desire to participate in project and work groups; and contribute to performance improvement.
- Responsibility — to achieve results within the set timeframe; to be ready to bear responsibility for failure to fulfill duties; to effectively balance personal objectives/results and the objectives/results of the company.
- Resourcefulness and capability to find non-routine solutions — to be internal entrepreneurs of the Company, generating new solutions and projects outside the range of standard duties, job functions or business based on either a new combination of traditional approaches and processes or their non-standard application.
- Loyalty — involvement in the activities of the company and its brand; avoidance of destructive negative criticism and readiness to participate in solution of company problems. All employees and managers are obliged to use company assets only for improvement and development of your company. Group's business and not for self-profit or individual career promotion.

- Focus on cooperation with fellow employees — readiness to participate in cross-functional teams and projects; giving positive and effective response to the requests of co-workers from other company divisions; readiness to share information. Efforts to establish barriers between divisions, competition for information and status, influence on functional divisions, sabotage of requests and appeals shall be considered destructive activity.

CHAPTER 5

Building the Business

Finding Clients

The business license is on the wall, the office is organized, all of the insurances are in place, the business cards are neatly placed in a holder on the desk and you are ready to get started. For many business owners, the easy part is behind them and now the work begins. If this is the first time you have ever been in business for yourself, the question that you are asking yourself at this point is – now what do I do?

The simple answer to this question is- start marketing and growing your business. But how do you grow a foreclosure business? All you need to get started is a computer, telephone and a commitment to spend the time necessary to build relationships with the people who will refer you the business. The property preservation business is all about relationships. If you are someone who does not like to speak with people on the phone this is probably not the business for you. In this chapter, I will share with you the best way to target the companies and people who will be the lifeblood of your success.

The Major Players

The Property preservation companies listed at the end of this chapter are currently some of the major players in the industry. This list contains companies with good track records of paying contractors for work completed properly and on time. When you decide to apply to become a vendor for a specific company it is important that you conduct your own due diligence by asking for specific information in writing. Important information that you need to receive should include;

- Copy of contract
- Payment Policies
- Invoicing procedures
- Technology/software requirements
- Required Job completion deadlines
- Picture policy

Be careful of fly by night companies. Many contractors across the country have been burned by companies that promise the world but never deliver the check! Mortgage Field Services is an unregulated industry and therefore is an industry that attracts unscrupulous types. Always do the necessary due diligence before you start working for any company. A few hours of research could save you thousands of dollars.

It is recommended you company focus your first efforts on the major national servicing companies. Most national servicing companies (nationals) have a revolving door of vendors. They are always recruiting new vendors to cover open areas. This will give you an opportunity to get business fairly quickly. The key is in knowing how to continue to get business from these companies.

The first step to becoming a vendor with a national servicing company is to visit their website and fill out the Vendor Application. It is very important that you fill this form out completely and accurately. Make sure that you have all of the required insurances, technology, equipment and staff in place to successfully fulfill the expectations set forth by the servicing company before submitting the vendor application. Once the application is submitted, most contractors sit back and wait for the company to contact them.

This is a big mistake. There are probably hundreds of other contractors submitting applications as well. Recruiters are overwhelmed with online applications and when you submit your application you have just become a number in a long list of numbers. Remember, I said that this is a relationship business? This is the time for you to make your application stand out and for you to begin a new relationship. Review the company's website and locate the name and phone number for the vendor manager responsible for your city, county, state or region. Sometimes this information will not be readily available and additional research will be required. I have used LinkedIn, Facebook, and numerous Property Preservation blogs and information sites to locate this information. Once you have the name and number of the Vendor Manager it is now time to call them directly on the phone and introduce yourself. Don't panic you can do this! The following is a sample template to use when speaking with the Vendor Manager for the first time.

> "Hello my name is (**name**) I am the owner of (**name of your company**) Preservation Company in (**city**) (**State**). I wanted to call and introduce myself and my company. I just completed and submitted the Vendor Application on line. I am very interested in becoming a vendor for your company. I can currently cover any needs you may have in (**whatever area you want to cover**). Do you currently have a need in this area?"

It is important that your company always ask if they have a need. In most cases they will have a need for a vendor. However, in large metropolitan areas they may already have enough vendors. Do not let this discourage you. This is actually an opportunity for you to fill the Vendor Managers needs and it could allow you the opportunity to get on board with the company. Let me explain, most property preservation contractors do not want to work outside of a fairly small radius. If you were one of the first vendors that signed up with the company this opportunity was available to you. Most likely this will not be the case. Don't be discouraged if the Vendor Manager informs you that there is no availability for new vendors in the area you want to focus on. I have made hundreds of thousands of dollars covering areas that no one else wanted to cover. Ask the Vendor Manager what areas are in need of contractors. Let the manager know that you would like the opportunity to see if you can cover that area for them. Also, ask that if you cover these areas would he be willing to also give you sufficient amount of work in your local area to help defer the cost of covering the outlying areas. This will show the Vendor Manager that you are serious about working as a team member and are willing to take the good work with the bad. Do not agree to cover areas that you are not sure that you can handle. Refer to the chapter regarding contractors for information on how to cover outlying areas. If you commit to cover an area and fail to do so you will lose the respect and confidence of the Vendor Manager and probably be fired. It is important to know your limits before you make the first call. After you speak with the Vendor Manager it is important that you immediately send a thank you note. Don't send a thank you e-mail. Everyone does this and e-mails a very impersonal form of communication. I always send a thank you card through the US mail. This takes a few days but very few people take the time to do this simple and important task. I will cover a program I like to use called Send Out Cards later in this chapter.

The process to become a vendor varies by company and can take anywhere from a few days to a few weeks before the boarding process is completed. In most cases once you become an official vendor you will be assigned to a regional vendor manager or regional representative. Depending on the company, this person will most likely be your point of contact for all communication regarding work load, adding or deleting territory coverage, policy and payment issues and other assistance you may need. This is the person that you will need to build your most important relationship with. It amazes me how many vendors never contact their Regional Managers and when they do it is usually to complain. Put yourself in the shoes of the Regional Manager. Would you want to get calls every day from vendors that just complain?

Develop a call schedule to stay in constant communication with your Vendor Manager. Make it a point to call your Vendor Manager at least twice a month. Be positive and ask how you can help them better serve their clients. The squeaky, happy wheel gets the grease in this business.

Local Reo (Real Estate Owned) Agents

REO Real Estate Agents are an excellent source of business for preservation contractors. There is a huge benefit to working with REO Agents – no percentage deduction! Working with REO Agents can be lucrative and is well worth a focused marketing effort to get them to use your company. As is the case with most good things in life, it takes hard work to secure this type of business.

Once again, relationships will determine if you are successful or not with REO Agents. If you think that all you have to do is call the agent on the phone, or just drop off a flyer at their office and they are suddenly going to give you business you will be disappointed. This is going to take a concerted effort on your part but the rewards are worth the effort.

First, you have to find REO Agents that work in your area. I have found the web site reoagents.net to be a good source for locating REO Agents across the country. Some areas may have 50+ agents or as few as one agent that specializes in REO properties. Once you identify the REO Agents in your area, the work of building that all important relationship begins. It is important to remember that banks, investors and financial institutions are the life blood for REO Agents. Just as a mother grizzly bear will go to all lengths to protect her cubs, a REO Agent will tolerate no mistakes by contractors that could jeopardize their relationship with the bank, investor or financial institution. An REO Agent will be very reluctant to use your company until they are comfortable with you and can trust your work. Most REO Agents that have been in the business for a significant amount of time will already have a list of preferred contractors that they use. How do you get on that preferred list? You have to become visible to the agent and you have to implement a consistent marketing effort and constantly ask for the business. On average, it takes 7 touches (contacts) before the average consumer will decide to give a specific company a try. The same is true with REO agents.

REO agents will have a need for several of your services. If you are a licensed contractor, in addition to performing basic property preservation services you may have the opportunity to perform complete home remodels to get the house ready for market.

Institutional Investors and Property Management Companies

Over the past several years' large institutional investors have been quietly buying up significant numbers of the existing foreclosed homes. In some cases, these investors have purchased thousands of homes in a single transaction. Now that these investors have these properties in their portfolio they need to prepare them for rent or sale. Property Preservation business owners willing to take the time to research these large institutional investor groups and the property management companies that handle their property portfolios have a excellent opportunity to secure significant business.

The following is a list of the type of jobs that you can expect to receive form these investor groups and property management companies;

- Interior and exterior remodeling
- Interior and Exterior painting
- Electrical repairs
- Plumbing repairs
- HVAC repairs/installation
- Concrete repair/replacement
- Water Damage repair
- Drywall repair
- Roof install/repair
- Meth/mold remediation
- Carpeting
- Window replacement/repair
- Siding, brick and stucco repair
- Yard clean-up
- Tree removal
- Sprinkler repair and installation
- Landscaping
- Kitchen Remodels
- Bathroom Remodels
- Trash removal
- Deep cleaning
- On-going yard maintenance

- On-going cleaning services
- On-going handyman services

How do you find these investors and Property Management companies? There are several ways to identify these groups. The following are some good suggestions for getting started.

- Search the internet for public announcements of large purchases of homes in your area.
- Contact local residential and commercial Real Estate Agencies and inquire if they are working with large institutional investors.
- Contact local property management companies and inquire if they are managing foreclosed properties for investors.
- Contact the County or local agency responsible for recording property purchase information. Research for significant purchases in your area.
- Contact Fannie Mae and Freddie Mack or visit their websites and ascertain any information on large purchase of homes from their property inventory by institutions or investors.

These are just a few ideas to get you started. They key to your success with these types of investors and management companies will be your persistence. Once you identify owners and management companies in your service area it is important that you are persistent in your marketing efforts. This group is business and market savvy and they have a proven system to maximize their profits. They know what it costs to paint a house, replace a roof, landscape a yard etc. They may also be working with a company that provides the same services you do. Do not be intimidated by this. It may be necessary for you to make 7-10 or more marketing visits before these groups give you an opportunity to prove yourself. Once you get that opportunity you have to be prepared to complete the job on time and professionally. Your goal is to have your company placed on their preferred vendor list.

List of Mortgage Field Service Companies

Mortgage Contracting Services
National Association of Housing and Redevelopment Officials (NAHRO)
National Default Servicing
National Field Network
National Field Representatives, Inc
National Vendor Management Services
Nationwide Field Inspectors
Nationwide REO Brokers
NewRep.com
NHS Contractors
NLA Management
North American Property Preservation
Northpoint Asset Management
Now Property Preservation
NREFSI
Ocwen Loan Servicing
Olympus Asset Management Inc
Pacific Preservation Services
Pennsylvania Housing Finance

3 Point Lender Services
A2Z Field Services
All REO Preservation Services
Altisource
America's Infomart
ASD America
Asset Management REO Marketing Services
Asset Management Specialists (AMS)
Asset One Marketing Group
Aurora Loan Services
Bank of America Supplier Relations
Best Assets
Chase Home Finance

Citimortgage
Cityside Management Corp
Coast2Coast Preservations
Commercial Property Preservation
Cooper-CitiWest
CW Capital
Cyprexx Services
Energy REO Solutions
Excellen REO
Fannie Mae
Field Asset Services
First American Field Services
First American Residential Value View
First Preston HC
Five Brothers Mortgage Company
Foreclosure Direct
Freddie Mac Homesteps
HSBC Mortgage Services
Department of HUD
Huntington Mortgage
Innotion
Keystone Asset Management
LAMCO Network
Laudan Properties, LLC
Leading Edge Companies
Litton Mortgage
LPS (aka Lender Processing Services)
Matt Martin Real Estate Management
Maxim Enterprises
MCBREO
Midland Mortgage
Miken Construction
M&M Mortgage Services
M&T Bank

PHH Mortgage
PK Management Group

PNC (formerly National City Bank)
Premier Field Services LLC
Reliance Field Services
REO Experts
REO Leasing Solutions
REO Preservation Services
RES.NET
RRI Field Services
Safeguard Properties
Sentinel Field Services, Inc
Spectrum Field Services
Suntrust Mortgage
Trash Out Pro
TREO Net
Trinity Real Estate Solutions
Universal Property Preservation
U.S. Best Repair Service
USA Property Preservation, Inc
Vault REO Service
Vendors Resource Management
White Van Real Estate Services LP

Chapter 6
HOW TO PERFORM MFS WORK

Key Phrases

Work Order Status
Work is to be completed by the due date indicated on the work order. If it is not possible to complete the work order within the allotted time frame – you must contact the YOUR COMPANY office. Sometimes work orders are forwarded to our office that are already past due, if you receive a work order where the due date is prior to the receive date please contact the YOUR COMPANY office to advise when you can complete this work order.

Cancelled Orders
Each morning, YOUR COMPANY sends out a list of cancellations that our clients have forwarded to us. Upon receipt of this list, please remove the cancelled work orders from your routing schedule. If you have completed the work order prior to our cancellation, call the office to inform them and update the information to us as soon as possible. We have 24 hours from receiving the cancellation to update it to the client in order to receive payment.

Invoice Procedures
It is the contractor's responsibility to ensure that all invoices are received within 8 hours of completion of the work order via the vendors web uploading.

When invoicing YOUR COMPANY, you must bill according to client pricing. Any additional information requested after the update is received must be received within 8 hours of the request. YOUR COMPANY will make every attempt to follow up in order to get this information updated. However, if the information is not received by the 1st day from completion date, YOUR COMPANY will decrease the Contractor's discount by 10% for the additional follow up required and it may result in less work. YOUR COMPANY reserves the right to return invoices unpaid when not received within the allotted time frame.

Updating Procedures
Updating our client as to when work is completed is one of YOUR COMPANY's most important functions. Contractors are required to update each completed job daily.

- Updates must include the date the work was completed. The completion date is important. Your clients will need the actual date work was completed in order to record deeds and quote figures for assumptions and reinstatements.
- Property condition reports must be filled out on the vendor web for all work orders with 24 hours of completion.
- It is imperative that all updates contain complete information regarding all completed work.
- Updates must always address damages. If there is no reference to damages on the update, the work order will remain open until that information is obtained. If damages are found, include a description and cause of damages as well as an estimate to repair.

Open Order/Incomplete Order Reports

Open order and incomplete order reports will be emailed to each contractor every week.

If an inquiry is emailed to you, it means that our vendor does not have all the information needed to close out an order. Please check to ensure your updates are complete and accurate the first time to avoid unnecessary delay and charge backs. You will receive reports from YOUR COMPANY to assist you.

- Responses to inquiries are needed within 24 hours. A work order will not be closed until YOUR COMPANY has all the required information to forward to our clients.
- Contractors will receive an Open Order Report once a week. The Open Order report contains a list of work orders for which YOUR COMPANY has not yet received an update. This report needs to be reviewed carefully. It is important that work is completed on time. After reviewing your open order report, forward completions back to YOUR COMPANY immediately. If there is any incorrect data, contact your YOUR COMPANY rep who will contact the Regional Coordinator so that it can be corrected.

Most common reasons that an order will remain open:
- Landfill receipt information not received
- Bid for roof work, but no estimate received for water damages
- Bid for mold damage, but no estimate received for water damages
- Photos supporting bid or second bid not received.
- Convey condition status not reported on convey orders.

- Insufficient detail on update.
- Property reported unsecure but no reason given or bid to secure received.
- No mention of utilities on if sum pump operational
- No mention of water off at the curb for winterization orders
- Lot size and grass height not mentioned on grass cut.

Photo Documentation

The amount of photos taken should tell the complete story of the property condition. No exceptions should be allowed. Please follow the documentation guidelines as noted for each work order, Client and office. No photos = no pay.

Photos are presented to our client with an invoice. All before, during and after photos must be taken from the same angle. Photo quality is very important. Blurry or distorted photos will not be accepted and will result in chargebacks.

Photo Guidelines:
- Photos must support all work performed and/or the bid submitted.
- If you are billing a charge and have no photos to support that charge, you will not be paid. If our client will not pay us, we will not be able to pay the Contractors for the work performed.
- Before, during and after photos are required for work completed.
- Please arrange the photos in a logical work order sequence when placing them on the web. For example, before showing window broken, during for half of the work completed and after showing window replaced.

- Photos must be taken in color and not black and white.
- It is recommended to not photo date stamp at the site and complete this process at the time of upload. This trick helps you out especially if you are given an extra day due to a holiday or certain weekends.

Since contractors use digital cameras to update photos directly to the website, please have contractors remove their camera of previous photos before transmitting to your company. Make sure you are renaming the new photos with the correct work order number. All your vendors have technology that can detect past photos. Attempts to replace old photos with current work order will result in non-payment and loss of work to contractors. There is a zero tolerance for using the same photos more than once.

- The photo(s), invoice and update must be put on the vendor web at the same time. This will result in quicker billing and more timely payment to the contractor.
- Landfill receipts put on the web must be designated as an update.
- When sending photos, please make sure all photos have a file size. Photos sent with no file size will transmit a blank photo that will need to be resent.

Locating Properties
Please make sure to inform us if there is a problem locating the property. Usually our clients will have a legal description on file that will facilitate locating the property. If the property still cannot be located, even after receiving the legal description, call our office immediately so that we can inform our client.

Below is a list of websites that can be consulted when a property has a bad address or is difficult to locate. It might be possible to avoid a long drive going nowhere if these sites are consulted before starting out or used to confirm property locations. They can also be used to check the validity of the addresses to be inspected that day.

www.usps.com
www.zillow.com
www.fedex.com
www.mapquest.com
www.expedia.com
www.mappointe.com
www.netronline.com

Many of will use a Garmin or Tom/Tom navigation system, but please make sure your company is still verifying the address before proceeding.

Trip Charges
When a trip is made to a property and work that is ordered cannot be completed (due to circumstances found at the property, i.e. occupied, active real estate listing, work performed by other, etc.), a contractor may submit an invoice for a trip charge. Every effort should be made to complete work while at the property so that trip charges can be kept to a minimum. Unforeseen circumstances will make it necessary to charge for a trip. If at any time you are unsure as to whether or not work should be completed, please contact the YOUR COMPANY office for assistance.

Quality Control Requirements
Taking time to ensure that you are fully addressing the needs of a property as they relate to the initial services is imperative. The

result of spending an additional 10 minutes at each property to ensure all the fixtures and rooms are cleaned properly as well as making sure your company performs yard maintenance properly will result in increased client satisfaction. Immediate improvement must be seen in this area by all vendors to ensure your company retains your REO volumes.

Gaining Access to Properties
It is extremely important to make sure you are at the correct address. Your company can only imagine the grief to all parties if the wrong property is entered. Make sure you are at the right property before you start.

Determining that a property is secure prior to our arrival is important. Read the work order to determine which door locks need to be changed. Upon arrival, assess whether the property is vacant – are any doors/windows standing open, any lights on, music/noise from inside, is the lawn being maintained, are there newspapers in the drive, mail in mail box, autos present with up to date plates, pets present, for sale sign present, etc.

Next, knock on the door (both front and back if you feel it necessary). If there is no answer, find the electric meter and see if it is moving (meaning electric is still on). If you are still uncertain, try to ask a neighbor or a mail carrier. If there is any doubt, call in and explain your concerns. If you enter the property and feel it is occupied, call the office for directions on how to proceed Note the condition of the door that requires a lock change, are there damages, is it locked etc. Take photo of entire door and frame showing the condition of door. Take a photo of the existing knob-lock and deadbolt (if present) before gaining access to property. Make sure to check all the doors and windows for possible access to the home. Only drill out the door lock(s) as a last resort to gain access. Note whether the property was secure upon arrival on the update. Check the property interior for personal property.

Should you encounter the occupant or homeowner, RESPECT THEIR PRIVACY, AVOID DISCRIMINATION, and AVOID CONFLICT? Keep in mind, the occupant may not be the homeowner. Keep the information you are privileged with confidential.

Personal Property
What happens if personals exceed $ amount after entering property?
Check the work order for the correct dollar amount of personals required. If estimated dollar amount of personals exceeds the amount listed on the work order call your office. Call your company office for directions and to notify them of the circumstances at the property. Check to see if the utilities are on or other indications the property is being maintained. Take condition photos of all sides of the house, outbuildings, yard, and every room in the house. Take photos of all the personal property present inside and outside of the house, include an estimate to remove (by cubic yard) and store the personals for 30 days (depending on state regulations). Check to see if the property is secure, i.e. open doors, unlocked windows, broken windows etc. Take photos of any additional doors, sliding glass door(s), shed(s), etc. that will require a lock change or padlock (per the work order) and provide a bid. Take photos of exterior and interior debris and provide a bid to complete the trashout and maid service. If the work order requests a winterization complete the winterization and take the appropriate photos to show your work (see winterization section before proceeding). If a grass cut is requested on the work order and the personal property or debris is not in the way of the grass cut, go ahead and perform the grass cut

and provide the appropriate photos to show your work (see yard maintenance section before proceeding). Go ahead and complete the lock change on the door you used to gain access, take the appropriate photos to show your work (see securing section before proceeding). Install the lockbox with the correct code and take the appropriate photos to show your work (see securing section). Look for interior and exterior damages or problems, take photos and provide bids. Provide bids and all information collected on update.

Personals do not exceed $ amount before entering house
Personal property generally means an item that is still in working/cosmetic condition, good enough to continue to use or be of value. Please refer to client guidelines for the dollar value of personal property that will determine whether the personal property will require storing for a period of time before disposal, or disposal during servicing the property. If the amount personal property present inside and outside of the home is less than what is listed on the work order proceed with work order.

Note: Determining and dealing with personal property can be difficult/risky. It seems that no matter how worthless the "left behinds" are, the owner may insist these items are very valuable. This could put you/your insurance at risk. The owner may want to be reimbursed for any items you remove from the property. There are safe/legal methods in dealing with personals and it has always been our position to error on the side of caution. Take a lot of pictures showing the honest condition of the property in question, inform your client and follow their instructions. You may find it tempting to salvage some of these personals for yourself, but please realize they may not be worth it in the long run. Itemize the property, set a value and keep yourself in a safe position.

Pricing Model
All clients have their own pricing structure. Please refer to the client allowables and/or regulations.

Verification of Vacancy
It is vital that a property be determined vacant prior to completing any work on the property. We are to use every means possible to verify the vacancy status of each property. These include, but are not limited to:
- Checking the utilities (are they on or off) How was this verified?
- Are personals visible? Where are they located-interior, exterior?
- What is the quantity (cubic yards) of the personals visible?
- What is the estimated value of any personals visible?
- Verify with a neighbor, postal carrier, etc. Try to obtain the name/address of the neighbor that information is verified with.
- Direct contact with occupant. Please try to obtain the name of the occupant.
- Is the property being maintained? – i.e., grass 4" tall, debris in yard, etc.
- Is the property unsecured and wide open?
- Is the property being renovated?
- If the property is for sale, please obtain the name/number of the realtor listing the property. Please obtain a photo
- If you have a question, call the YOUR COMPANY rep and ask them to contact the regional coordinator before entering the property.

Securing Requirements

All REO and Property Preservation properties must be secured and winterized (where/when applicable) within 48 hours. Door locks are to be changed (as per customer request), including deadbolts (cover plates should not be used) – unless the work order advises otherwise. If the securing will take you over the allowable, you must call your local YOUR COMPANY office to contact the regional coordinator from the site.

Low Impact Access

Spend a few minutes looking over the security of the house to decide which door or window (sometimes you will find an unsecured window) to attack. It is better to approach a door with just a knob set than a door with two locks. Dead bolts are much more time-consuming than a knob set. An unsecured window, however, is usually the fastest approach.

Note: It is rare, but being approached by the authorities due to a report by a watchful neighbor happens. Always have a copy of your work order and all the proper credentials for you and your vehicle.

When breaching a knob set, grasp the outside knob with channel lock pliers; apply increasingly firm pressure while slowly twisting the knob. Also, while twisting the knob, apply gentle but increasing pressure on the door itself with your shoulder. Normally, twisting the knob will break or override the internal parts of the lock and allow the door to open. If this doesn't work, you will need to disassemble the knob one layer/part at a time until it no longer secures the door. Do not damage the door while dismantling the lock or you will be liable to replace the door. Once you have dismantled a lock once or twice, you may still find it aggravating, but not too terribly time consuming.

To dismantle a knob set, use your drill with a 3/16" bit (any one of two or three bits close to that size will do – hopefully your bit is sharp). Place the bit in the center of one of the areas to the left or right of and horizontal with the knob. (If you will inspect a new lock from your inventory, the location of these screws will be readily apparent and since most knob sets you will encounter will be KwikSet, this drilling method should be fairly typical of most locks. Drill out these two screws, drilling about 2" deep and the lock should come apart, with the inside parts falling to the floor. This will expose the bolt so it can be slid out of the strike/jamb, allowing the door to swing open.

IMMDEIATELY AFTER BREACHING THE DOOR, IT IS VERY IMPORTANT TO LOUDLY ANNOUNCE YOUR INTENT TO ENTER THE HOUSE. IF NO ANSWER, ENTER.

Hint: Some deadbolts have one or more of the mounting screws that are hardened, making them difficult/impossible to drill. Normally, you only want to deal with a dead bolt as a last resort. If you cannot drill a dead bolt but are forced to remove it, begin by starting a tear in the brass skin and continuing to rip the brass skin off until the cast metal ring underneath is exposed. This metal ring can then be split, using a sharp cold chisel. After splitting/removing the metal ring, the bolt is exposed and can then be disassembled one part at a time, until you can slide the bolt out of the strike/jamb.

Notes:

Once in a while, you may encounter a lock of a different brand. Just use common sense and proceed. Breaching an odd lock now and again is part of becoming proficient at your trade, so embrace the challenge with gusto.

When working for a client that approves the practice, try to salvage the undamaged/working locks from the house and re-key these locks for use at the client's next property (once trained, this becomes excellent work for a teenager – it teaches mechanics and allows them to make extra money). It is rare to find keys for these salvaged locks; therefore, these locks must be "blown-out" to re-key. This means you must take the cap off of the top pin chamber and landfill out all top pins, springs and bottom pins, before the tumbler can be removed. Once you have removed the tumbler, you must rebuild the tumbler system.

To rebuild the tumbler system, you must insert the follower tool in the tumbler (pointed in the proper direction), select the five top pins from the pile of pins and springs you have removed (the top pins will be the five short pins that all look exactly alike and flat on both ends – line all of them up side by side to be sure). Once you have selected the five top pins, insert them in the top pin chamber, followed by the five companion springs (special care should be used in replacing the springs in order to keep one of them from flying away – if one of the springs should be lost, retrieve an extra from your miscellaneous parts bottle and continue). After the pins and springs are in, re-install the chamber cap. Make sure all the springs are compressed down straight in their holes and that both sides of the chamber cap are snapped down firmly.

Next, re-pin the tumbler and complete the re-key assembly process. After you have performed this a few times, it will be easy to accomplish in about two minutes. Put the old pins and extra parts into your miscellaneous parts container. Further, since you may bear the cost of returning to a property if the door lock doesn't work for another party, you should make sure the inside of a re-keyed lock is well lubricated.

Install Lock Box
Lockboxes are to be installed unless it is not stated on the work order to install. Once you have completed the lock change(s) per the work order a lock box must be installed. Check the work order for the lock box combination required for that property. You will install the lock box on the main door or the door that you completed a lock change on. Take a photo of the door before installing the lock box (after the lock change was completed), take a photo of the door with the lockbox in place with lockbox open and working keys inside, a take a photo up close of the lockbox code so you can read the code. This last photo will show that we installed the correct lockbox and code. Make sure you put the proper keys inside for all the locks installed on the property. On the update we need to know the lockbox code and where it was installed.

Securing Photos

- Before photo showing old mechanism in place.
- During photo showing old mechanism removed.
- After photo showing new mechanism installed.
- Lockbox showing keys placed inside.
- Photo showing the for sale sign if present on the property.

Door Knob Install Before

Door Knob Install During

Door Knob Install After

The Property Preservation Coach

Deadbolt Install Before

Deadbolt Install During

Deadbolt Install After

Lockbox Install Before

Lockbox Install During

Lockbox Install After

Garage Doors

If the house has an overhead garage door, find a hole in the side track (as close to the floor as possible) that will accept a padlock. Snap a padlock in place in such a manner as to not allow the overhead door to raise enough for an intruder to crawl under.

Boarding Requirements

When determining whether to board a property, the contractor must follow the client specific guidelines on each work order. Most initial services orders give pre-approval to board if needed. There are emergency allowable for some clients if boarding costs will be high. The important thing is to never leave a property unsecure. If unsure on how to proceed with regard to boarding, always call your local YOUR COMPANY rep to call the regional coordinator from the site.

All boarding must be completed to the required standard (pricing and completion requirements) – nail and screw boarding is not permitted. Dimensions must always be reported and all broken glass must be removed as part of the boarding fee.

How to Board

Measure the required size of plywood, 2x4s, and bolt hole locations. Cut and drill your materials. (This method is for boarding with only one man. If using two men, it is not necessary to measure for the bolt holes). If only one man is present, insert the carriage bolts through the drilled bolt holes and place plywood in position. The bolts will over balance to the inside and generally hang in place until you are ready to insert the bolts through the 2x4s after they are positioned on the inside of the window. Lightly nail the plywood in place as to not damage the window frame or trim.

Position the top 2x4 to align with the top two carriage bolts and lightly nail in place, paying attention not to cause too much damage to the inside fascia. Next, position the bottom 2x4 in place to accept the two lower carriage bolts. Insert the bolts through the holes in the 2x4, add the washers/nuts, and tighten securely.

If a two man crew is used, do not pre-drill plywood or 2x4s. One man can hold plywood in place over the window opening from the outside, while the other man holds one 2x4 in place and drills through 2x4 and plywood with a 16" x 7/16" bit. BE CAREFUL NOT TO DRILL INTO THE OUTSIDE MAN'S HANDS. The outside man can then insert bolts through plywood and 2x4s. The inside man helps to align the bolts as they are pushed through by the outside man, and he will install washers/nuts and tighten. Repeat this process for the second 2x4. Even with a one man crew, it should take no more than 10 – 15 minutes to board a normal sized first floor window. Boarding a second floor window is a little more complicated, but is normally able to be accomplished from inside the house. Second story boarding should be approved by the Client before proceeding. To board a second floor window from the inside, cut the plywood and 2x4s to size, lay the plywood on a flat surface outside, position the 2x4s on top of the plywood in their pre-measured positions, (it is important to drill the bolt holes where the bolts will not encounter an obstacle when inserted) and drill through both the 2x4 and plywood at the same time. This will ensure that the holes match. Next, carry the materials inside to the window, insert all four carriage bolts through the plywood, and position the plywood to slide outside through the window opening on the diagonal. This may require the gentle removal of one or more of the trim strips inside the window opening, to allow clearance for the plywood to pass through to the outside. Once outside, the plywood can be held and maneuvered into position by holding onto the carriage bolts previously inserted through the plywood. After positioning the plywood, the bolts can be inserted through the corresponding holes in the 2x4s, receive the washers/nuts and be tightened in place. This method sounds complicated and is a bit more difficult, but is much faster and safer than having one man work off of a ladder outside. Again, after completing a few boarding's, the process will become much easier.

Sliding Glass Door Boarding Before

Sliding Glas Door Board During

Sliding Glass Door Boarding After

Window Boarding Before

Window Boarding During

Window Boarding After

Re-glazing

From time to time you will find windows that are not secured due to damage, missing locks, broken panes, etc. Broken panes will be handled through client guidelines as to whether the window is to be boarded or re-glazed. If it is to be boarded, see the "boarding" in this section. Replacing a broken pane is simple once a person has been shown the proper method and has acquired the proper tools and materials. The tool is nothing more than a ¾ inch wood chisel – it doesn't even have to be sharp. The materials consist of a pint can of painter's putty and a small box of glazier's points. The procedure is merely getting a piece of single strength glass cut to fit, getting the old glass out (be advised that there are generally a few small metal "arrowheads" driven into the wooden window mull. These arrowheads (glazier's points) are laying flat against the glass and sealed away under the old window putty. These points must be removed before installing the new glass (just flick them out with the corner of your wood chisel). After the new glass is in place, new points should then be installed to secure the new pane, before the new putty is installed over the new pane. It is suggested that your handy man be able to glaze or have him ask for a brief training from a local glass shop. Don't panic, it's easy after you have completed two or three. Should you find a window that has its lock missing, is out of alignment, or damaged enough that the lock won't catch, you should drive a 2" or 3" sheet rock screw into the side frame just above the top of the bottom sash to keep the bottom sash from being raised, or just below the bottom of the top sash to prevent the top sash from being lowered. This will secure the window until proper repairs can be made.

Winterization Requirements

Winterizations are to be completed as shown in the attachment. **Be sure to refer to the most current winterization memos for proper procedures.** Remember that all water must be completely drained, including the water in sinks (P-Traps), toilet bowls and tanks, water heaters and water softeners. If the property is found to be frozen upon arrival, you must provide a bid to thaw. This includes the number of portable heaters required, number of man hours required, and a bid to pressure test the system for leaks once thawed. Also include the cost to winterize the property once thawed. If a winterization is requested on your work order this section needs to be filled out whether you completed the winterization or not. Circle whether the winterization was: complete, partial, N/A, intact, or bid. A partial winterization can be completed by putting antifreeze in the traps and/or draining the water heater when there are plumbing breaks, frozen water lines, missing plumbing lines or fixtures, etc. We also REQUIRE the status of the utilities upon arrival and upon departure with pictures showing number on the gas, water and electrical meters. Was the gas on or off upon arrival, what is the meter reading, what is the serial number for the meter, and was the gas on or off upon departure. Was the electric on or off upon arrival, what is the meter reading, what is the serial number for the meter, and was the electric on or off upon departure. Was the water on or off upon arrival, what is the meter reading, what is the serial number for the meter, and was the water on or off upon departure. At every property we need to check for a sump pump, if a sump is found check to see if the sump pump is operable. If the sump pump is not operable bid to repair or replace the sump pump.

Steps to winterize

1. Make sure water is turned off at the main or at the utility meter. Treat the water meter per client guidelines and state/local regulations (whether to be removed or not).
2. Connect a garden hose to the drain valve of the water heater and open the valve. Make sure the hose is long enough to reach outside the house, and far enough from the house to not let the water run back under the house or in the basement.
3. Check all other faucets/valves to make sure they are closed (including supply stops at all toilets).
4. Connect air compressor to hot water side of washer/dryer connections. (If no washer/dryer connections, connect to any faucet or hose bib available.) Turn on compressor to begin charging system.
5. After water heater empties, close drain valve and supply stops at each toilet.
6. Begin systematically opening a faucet at the highest level of the house. Leave faucet open until water stops emitting from that faucet. Close that faucet and go to the next faucet and repeat until all faucets have been drained.
7. Go to each bath room in turn and add RV (non-toxic) anti-freeze into both the toilet tank and bowl in sufficient amount to prevent these areas from freezing per your local winter conditions. While in each bath room, add the same anti-freeze to all traps/drains present. Go the each other bath room and repeat. Go to the kitchen and add same anti-freeze to both sides of the kitchen sink and dishwasher and

any other traps/drains in the kitchen. Further, add the same anti-freeze to every other trap/drain, such as but not limited to, washer drain, evaporator drain, floor drain, etc.

Hint: Remove all water from toilet tanks and bowls. If there is water standing in the bowl, we further suggest to pour approximately 3 gallons of water into the bowl fast enough to cause the bowl to flush itself. When it flushes properly, there will be very little water left in the bowl.

Note: Pay strict attention to the taking of all photographic documentation and the placement of all warning/informational notices per client requirements.

DRY HEAT SYSTEMS – The water supply to the property should be shut off at the curb. If curb shut off is not possible, the main interior water supply must be shut off. In either case, the water meter must be disconnected and left in the property unless the City or County ordinance requires return of the meter to the water company to eliminate further water charges. The disconnected feed pipe leading from the main water valve must be plugged. Tags, labels, or warning signs must be affixed to all items winterized and must include the date of winterization and the name, address, and telephone number of the firm that performed the work. For properties with wells, the pump (if not submersible) and tank must be drained. The hot water heater and all domestic supply and distribution piping must be thoroughly drained. All faucet and valves must be opened in the process and then closed after draining is completed. Toilets must be cleaned before winterization materials are used. Use of air pressure to clear the system or, in some cases, adding anti-freeze to the systems are both acceptable provided that the effect is prevention of freeze-ups. Adequate amounts of anti-freeze are to be placed in all fixture traps including toilet tanks and bowls. All winterization must be performed in accordance with state and local codes, ordinances and regulations.

WET HEAT, RADIANT, HYDRONIC OR HOT WATER BASEBOARD SYSTEMS – The winterization requirements outlined above for domestic water apply except that water should not be shut off to or in the property. Test for system security. Pressurize the system with an air compressor to 35 pounds and inspect for leakage. System must hold air pressure with no leakage for a minimum of one-half hour.
Drain the boiler and all heating loops. Repair, replace, or install (as necessary to comply with state health department requirements) a Reduced Pressure Zone (RPZ) valve. Such a valve shall be installed between the furnace and the main feed water supply, adjacent to the furnace.

Fill the boiler and all heating loops with a non-toxic anti-freeze (propylene-glyol) solution designated for hot water heating systems (with anti-rust ingredient) tested to a freeze point of –40 degrees Fahrenheit, or lower. Isolate loops or bleed in sequence to ensure proper flushing through the lines. Bleed all vents in the system to ensure that all air has been voided from the system.
Return the heating system to normal operating temperature and pressure. Check the entire system for proper operation. Leave heat on. Tape the furnace electrical switch to the "on" position. Tape card above the switch stating, "Do Not Remove Tape. Do Not Turn Off."
Set the thermostat at 55-degrees. In the event major repair or replacement would be necessary in order to make the heating system operational, contact the M&M contractor for instructions.

STEAM HEAT SYSTEMS – The winterization requirements outlined above for domestic water apply. Determine if the system is operable and if there are any leaks. Report this information to the M&M contractor. In addition, the house boiler system must be thoroughly drained. All radiator vents are to be opened in the process and bleeder pins must not be removed from the radiators.

HOT WATER BASEBOARD HEAT SYSTEMS – As a point of clarity HUD considers that hot water baseboard heat is separate and distinct from heating derived from steam heat systems and dry heat systems. For the point of this discussion, hot water baseboard heating systems derive heat from hot water carried through copper tubing (normally 3/8 inches to ¾ inch diameter, however tubing can be as wide as 1 ½ inches in diameter).

Securing Pools

Typical Abandoned Pool

Per HUD requirements, pools must be covered with a frame consisting of 2x6 joists, 6"x6" woven wire and polyethylene. The specifications are available in the HUD Guidelines. The difficult part of these requirements is that some pools do not have an apron large enough to build the system on the apron and then slide it out over the pool. You may have to build the frame in the yard and then maneuver it into the pool area to install. If necessary, after the frame is installed, use a 2'x4'x1/2" piece of plywood to crawl out onto the bare frame to install the woven wire and plastic sheeting. This is not recommended, but sometimes necessary to complete the work.

HUD Requirements to secure pool

1. Remove all water except four feet or whatever depth may be required by local authorities.
2. Add chlorine to the water.
3. Drain the pool pumps, filters and lines.
4. Install any pool cover that may be present.
5. Cover the pool with a wood frame, poly sheeting and then wire mesh. Do not use the poly sheeting in Arizona, California, Hawaii, Nevada or the Pacific Islands.
6. Secure pool gates with padlock.
7. Repair any damaged fencing around the pool.

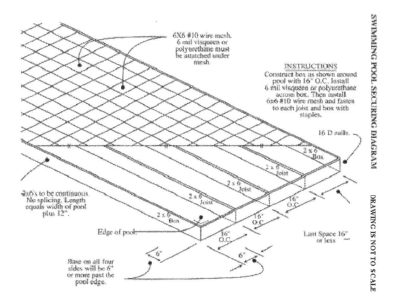

Debris Removal & Trashout Services

Measuring and Billing for General Debris

Measuring is sometimes difficult. As you are aware, a cubic yard is 3'x 3'x3'. A normal washer or dryer is considered approximately 1 cubic yard each. It is difficult to estimate yardage when there seems to be debris everywhere. One method is to start inside the house with a pad and pencil. Go to the first room and imagine how much there is when compared to a washer or dryer. Write your estimate down on your pad and add up all the amounts when finished inside. After completing the interior, do the same for the exterior – again comparing the different piles to a washer or dryer. Then add all the numbers together to get total yardage for the job. Keep in mind that some customers require you to separate all interior, exterior, hazardous and non- hazardous trash, get into the habit of separating your count into these categories; it will make it easier during your uploading and bidding process. Try to charge according to the HUD Regulations for your area whenever possible. Be sure to check all attics, crawl spaces, and behind outbuildings. When there are woods surrounding the property, it is important to check if debris has been thrown in the woods. Remember, the more debris you find, the more you make (if properly estimated). Your ability to estimate cubic yardage should improve with experience. It is better to error on the high side. It is better to over bid and lose the job than to underbid and lose money.

Disposal of Debris/Haz-Mats
All hazardous material should be segregated from normal debris per the restrictions of your local disposal facility. Dry metal items (all fluids/oils/fuels removed) can be sold to your local recycle company facility if these items weigh enough to warrant the extra handling. All Haz-Mats *must* be disposed properly at approved facilities, per local, state, and federal regulations. It would be prudent to spend some time looking for the facilities in your area that will take (and maybe even pay for) some of these extra money items instead of having to pay the fees other facilities sometime charge. Be creative, this material can be expensive to dispose of, know your costs.

Paint
There are some creative solutions to disposing of paint. Here are some options for you to consider:

- Sell it on Craigslist.

- Save the white or cream colors to paint over vandalism.
- Charity Drives will take this for no charge.
- Dispose of it at a landfill. Most landfills require that all paint be "dried". To dry the paint quickly, mix it with a material such as floor dry or kitty litter. Both of these products can be salvaged from houses and stored until needed. If material of this type is not available, you can either buy the material or partially fill a garbage bag with rags/discarded clothing and empty approximately ½ gallon of liquid paint into a bag. If the bag is left to sit/soak for a while before taken to the landfill, it should be acceptable.

Performing the Trash Out

Waste materials, debris, and rubbish must be removed from the premises and properly disposed of. Do not use city trash pickup services for debris removal. Use only environmentally safe cleaners. Use deodorizers and air fresheners that contain lemon, floral or pine scent. In addition, all hooks nails and draperies must be removed from wall on REO properties. Once you have completed the exterior and interior evaluations of the property and you have taken all the before debris removal photos continue with the trash out. When removing exterior debris, the contractor must assure every piece of paper and trash is removed from the yard. Each time you fill the trailer or truck take a photo of the rear of the empty trailer or truck in front of the property and photos of employees filling the trailer or truck and another photo of the trailer or truck full in front of the property before going to the dump. When removing exterior debris watch for trip hazards or holes, you may want to include these in your bid. Once all the debris is removed go back and take the after photos of the debris removed. Remember to stand in the same spot as the before photo for the after photo and the number of before and after photos should match. When removing interior debris make sure that you remove everything from the shed, barns, garages etc. If you are removing something that you can charge extra for, take a before and after photo of that item separate from the items around it, this would include items such as tires, appliances, large furniture, bags of cement, bricks, cinder blocks etc. Each time you fill the trailer or truck take a photo of the rear of the empty trailer or truck in front of the property and photos of employees filling the trailer or truck and another photo of the trailer or truck full in front of the property before going to the dump. Once all the debris is removed go back and take the after photos of the debris removed. Remember to stand in the same spot as the before photo for the after photo and the number of before and after photos should match.

Trash Removal
Empty Trailer–At property

Trash Removal
At Property - Full

Trash Removal at Dump

Trash Removal During

Trash Removal at Landfill   Trash Removal Empty Trailer

REO Maid Services

Ensuring that a property is in marketable condition and appealing to buyers is of the utmost importance. Maid service must be done in a very thorough manner and inspected by the contractor upon completion. Below is a listing of the tasks involved in a thorough maid service cleaning. IF THE PROPERTY IS WINTERIZED DO NOT POUR ANY WATER DOWN ANY SINK, TOILET, TUB, SHOWER OR ANY DRAIN ON THE PROPERTY. It is always recommended to carry your own water for cleaning and winterized property.

- Clean all baseboard, doors, light-switches and outlet covers, light fixtures including ceiling fans, and heat and air vents/duct covers. Remove any dirty non-washable window covers
- Clear cobwebs from ceilings, walls, light fixtures, fans windows, doors, entryways, porches and walkways.
- Clean all kitchen and bathroom counter tops, cabinets, and drawers to remove dirt, smudges, grim and debris. Leave drawers and cabinets open until final inspection.
- Clean sinks and appliances through premises.

- Clean kitchens and bathrooms thoroughly, including all fixtures and surfaces using a disinfectant cleaner to remove dirt, grime mildew and odor.
- Clean toilets, toilet bowls and surrounding areas thoroughly. Tape down toilet seat lids on winterized properties when finished.
- Clean full-view glass doors at front and rear entries. Clean interior side of glass in windows to remover dirt, grime, fingerprints, tape, stickers, etc. Clean window ledges to remove dirt, smudges, cobwebs, insects and grime.
- Broom sweep interior floors, wet mop vinyl floors and vacuum carpeted floors and rugs to present neat appearance. Be sure to include stairs, closets, baseboards and other similar areas.
- Place one air freshener in kitchen and one in each bathroom.
- Pine, floral and lemon scents are acceptable.
- Broom-sweep all porches, garages and carports and entries leading into property to present a neat appearance.
- Sweep out fireplaces and remove ashes or residue. Close the damper.
- Pick up and properly dispose of all debris from interior, including miscellaneous trash on porches and in closets and cabinets.
- Remove all broken glass from any broken windows and board the windows.

REO Maid Services Photo Requirements
- Before, during and after pictures of each room in the house.

- Before, during and after pictures of the windows being washed inside and out.
- Before, during and after pictures of all outside entry ways that are swept.
- Before, during and after pictures of the lockbox to show proof keys were replaced in lockbox.
- <u>7 pictures</u> of any new property damage since last visit (broken windows, stolen appliances etc. call your company office from site for further instructions).

REO Maid Services Contract Checklist

All items must be initialed and the form must be signed at the bottom. This is a required part of your work order and it must be submitted. Please see attached.

As a reminder, you must call the listing agent and advise when the trash out and maid services have been completed. It is imperative that contractors do so, as the agents then need to inspect the property and fill out the broker sign off sheet. Please see attached.

REO Maid Service Refresh

This is a service offered on REO properties or for REO agents. In order to efficiently and effectively complete the maid refresh services, in some cases contractors will be required to maintain a maid refresh list (similar to the grass cut list) and utilize a separate maid service crew to perform the service.

- Work order instructions include the following:
- Wipe down counters and cupboards
- Clean windows and window sills
- Clean all sinks, tubs and toilets.
- Vacuum carpets

- Mop floors
- Replace all air fresheners

Call from site to obtain approval for any of the following that may be needed and be prepared to do the work:
- Securing
- Debris Removal
- Shrubs
- Grass
- Emergency Repairs

REO Maid Service Refresh Photos Requirements

The following maid service refresh photos are required:
- Each refresh will require a minimum of 35 photos; as many during photos as needed per work completed, with before, during and after photos.
- Mandatory photos on each order will be the water meter, all toilets with lids up and main water valve zip tied in the off position to ensure the winterization is still intact (if allowed by local ordinances).
- All flat surfaces must be wiped down with cleaning chemicals. All floors, carpets must be vacuumed and hard surfaces must be mopped as needed. Please include a photo of all sinks and tubs to ensure they are in a clean condition.
- If a room is clean and does not need a refresh, a general condition photo of the entire room from opposite angles is needed to ensure proof that further cleaning is not needed.

Light Bulb Replacements (REO properties only)
In order to ensure that properties show well, it is imperative that light bulbs are replaced in common areas. Please follow the instructions below when addressing light bulbs in REO properties:

If electricity is off or on:
- Replace any missing light bulbs in common areas listed below:
- Interior are basement, bathrooms, bedrooms, dining rooms, family/living rooms, hallways, kitchens, stairways.
- Exterior areas are entryways to house, front porch, and security lights.
- Supply pictures to support work.

Lawn Maintenance

Cut lawn to property edge and to a maximum height of 3 inches, or to requirements of local code or consistent with surrounding properties, unless otherwise instructed by your company. All grass clippings must be removed from the lawn, sidewalks, steps, etc.

Trim shrubs away from the house, walkways and entrances unless over allowable, if over allowable please submit a bid. Sweep or otherwise clear all paved surfaces. <u>Edge all paved surfaces</u> and trim around all trees, bushes, fences, foundations, sprinkler heads and planting beds.

Grass Cut Only Work Orders
Verify property address and if vacant. Cut lawn to property edge and to a maximum height of 3 inches, or to requirements of local code or consistent with surrounding properties, unless otherwise

instructed by your company. All grass clippings must be removed from the lawn, sidewalks, steps, etc.

Grass cut work orders do not give permission to the inside of the property. DO NOT go inside the property under any condition. If you notice new damage to a property or the property is unsecure (broken window) call you company immediately.

Grass Cut Photo Requirements
- Must have a picture of the front of the property.
  *Take an additional picture of the cross street in rural areas.
- Before, during and after photos are required to be taken from the same angle.

Grass Cut Before Photos

Grass Cut During Photos

Grass Cut After Photos

Repairing Fences

Bids for fence repairs will vary depending on the size/type of fence and the section that needs to be repaired. Contractors are required to supply the length of fencing to be replaced, the height of the fence, and the type/material of the fence.

Snow Removal

Snow removal is ordered by brokers on an as needed basis and must be completed within 48 hours. Snow removal is to be completed with city ordinances with walkways and sidewalks to be cleared. Please read the work order carefully.

Providing Bids

All bids must be justified with photo documentation and complete descriptions of the work that must be performed. New photos must always be provided on work per bid completions.

Firearms & Illegal Substances

If you encounter weapons/ammunition when performing work on a property, please be sure to contact your local law enforcement agency immediately to inquire how they would like you to handle the removal of these items. The process varies depending on the jurisdiction in which the property is located. Some areas require these items be removed by the authorities, other areas require we report the items to the client before storing them so there is record. Finally other areas advise us to leave them in the home and we will in turn report the items to the client as personals. In all scenarios, it is required to report the contact name and phone number at the police department and to document their conversation with the authorities under the comments section.

Legal Complaints

Occasionally complaints may be received from mortgagors or neighbors of properties. Your company maintains a neutral position by acting as an intermediary. It makes no judgments, gives opinion, or makes assumptions about any complaints received. It is important that contractors respond to the complaint within 24 hours to allow your company and our vendor to provide updates to clients and complainants in a timely manner. The questions need to be answered as accurately and completely as possible and any additional comments can be added for clarification and explanation. The Legal Department would appreciate contractor's written update to be sent via email and asks that contractors refrain from placing phone calls to reduce delays and interruptions. If a contractor fails to replay to the request for information within the allotted time, checks for that week may be held until the information is received.

Property Stickers

Photos are required of all posted stickers. Stickers are to be placed on glass surfaces. Care should be taken as to not cover any vacancy stickers.

A photo must be taken of the posted sticker. Do not place stickers on wooden surfaces. Do not cover the vacancy sticker that has been left by field inspectors. These stickers are dated and the date needs to remain visible.

Vacant Mobile/Manufactured Homes

When performing any maintenance work order on a mobile or manufactured home and you are reporting it as vacant, the VIN # must be obtained and provided on the update. This information is mandatory for our clients and we have committed to them that it will be provided on all vacant properties.

Where to find the VIN Number

Mobile homes will have the serial number or VIN placed at more than one location. The serial number or VIN could be inside the mobile home in a kitchen or utility cabinet, by the electrical circuit breaker box, under the tongue, on the tongue, underneath the mobile home, or on a plate near the front or back door. If the data plates that are supposed to be inside the unit have been removed, the serial number or VIN can be located on the tow bar/hitch or frame front cross member of each transportable section. Usually it is cold stamped directly onto the outside of a steel crossbeam that is part of the main undercarriage frame.

Emergency Repairs

Report any hazardous, unsafe, or unsecure conditions at the property to YOUR COMPANY so that we can call the regional coordinator from the site. If there is an emergency repair such as standing water in a basement or an active roof leak, call from site. Always advise on the specifics of the damages, such as location, dimensions of affected areas, bids to tarp and repair/replace etc. Always take at least 7 pictures of the damaged area.

Bids & Allowables

It is important to know what types of items our customers want us to bid on, listed are some of the categories and all bids will fall under one of these.

- Safety – We want to identify and bid on all items that are related to safety for the property or for personal safety. Look for missing:

  Smoke detectors, co2 detectors, open water piping, hanging drywall and /or ceilings, exposed wires (live/powered off), non-capped gas lines, loose carpet/vinyl (tripping hazards), broken steps/handrails, open septic tank holes, yard holes, outlet / switch covers, over hanging bushes / trees or touching roof, water heaters pressure relief valves, holes in firewalls etc.

- Securing – All windows, doors, gates and openings on all buildings, sheds and outbuildings should be secured including crawl spaces under foundations and under mobile and manufactured homes.

- Violation – local municipalities usually have a "code enforcement" division; they are tasked to monitor, among other things, the foreclosed properties in the city to ensure the property does not become a safety or eyesore issue. Fines for these violations are very large. Items that are looked for are overgrown grass, weeds, tumble weeds. Broken windows, unsecured doors, unsecured yards and pools and any other item that presents a hazard to the property, community or self. Always bid on these items and use the phrase "to avoid violation" in the bid this will prompt action from the bank so they do not get fined. When a property has a violation against it, code enforcement will post the violation on the front door. Take a picture of the violation and call your company from the site for further direction.

- Preservation – These are non-emergency or safety issues generally will pertain to items that need to be done to keep the property in its current condition or stop damages from happening while in process. Examples are:

Roofs, siding, tree and shrub trimming, tumbleweed removal, window and door replacement and /or boarding, winterizations, cover swamp coolers, pest control.

- Marketable Conditions – These repairs will help the value of the house, help the house to sell faster and generally upgrade the current condition. Do not bid unless requested on the work order. Examples are:

Interior / exterior painting including fascia, carpet cleaning, removal or replacement, repair damaged walls / ceilings or any general repair to improve the property.

Pest Control

Exterminations are needed if the property shows evidence of infestation by snakes, rodents, fleas, roaches and/or ants or any other pest that should not be in or around the house and property. Most infestations require a licensed exterminator in which a bid must be submitted with an actual estimate from the licensed exterminator.

When invoicing for the extermination you must have before, during and after photos including photos of the vehicle, exterminator and equipment. It is best to take a picture of the vehicle in front of the location. Make sure you add a trip charge to the invoice for your time involved in taking the pictures.

Pest Removal – Bees
Before

Pest Removal – Bees
Before

Pest Removal – Bees
During

Pest Removal – Bees
After

Pest Removal – Bees
After

Pest Removal – Bees
After

Vehicle Removal

It is mandatory to supply written and photo proof of the make, model, color, VIN #, license plate # and current tag status with all vehicle removals.

Vehicle Removal
Before

Vehicle Removal
Before - Plates

Photo of tags

Vehicle Removal
Before - VIN

Vehicle Removal
Before - VIN

Local laws will determine how to proceed. Contact your local Sheriff's office for regulations. There are some tow companies who will do the paperwork required by your state when they remove the vehicle.

Bidding on Vehicle Removal

Before removing any vehicle know your local laws. If your cost to remove a vehicle exceeds the allowable a bid must be submitted, a valid reason for the bid must be given and a receipt must be provided. Before, during and after pictures are required for each vehicle, remember to include pictures of the tow truck and employee removing the vehicle/s. If you are required to store the vehicle provide all information as to where the vehicle is located including address and phone number.

If a contractor is bidding over the allowable for vehicle removal, they must provide a valid reason why the removal cannot be done for the allowable.

Vehicle Removal Picture Requirements

Vehicle Removal Address

Vehicle Removal Before

Vehicle Removal Before

Vehicle Removal Before

Vehicle Removal Before

Vehicle Removal Before

Vehicle Removal During

Vehicle Removal After

**Copy of Towing
Company Receipt**

Roof Patching or Repair

Any time a property has a roof leak, we require a bid to patch or repair the leak as a solution to prevent further damage, unless the patch or repair can be completed for the allowable stated on the work order.

- Include with your bid or update: 1) the size of the area to be patched, repaired or tarped and 2) the type or repair and materials to be used. Photos of the specified areas are required with the bid. If a patch, tarp or repairs are completed submit before, during and after photos.
- Be specific as to what area of the roof is being addressed (front, back, entire roof etc.).
- If a roof cannot be patched or repaired for the allowable, it should be tarped and provide a bid to patch or repair. Before you tarp, call your company office first to see if we

can get approval for the additional cost of the repair or patch.
- Flat roofs should never be tarped. The tarp could result in more damage call your company office from the site for further instructions.
- If the roof leak resulted in interior wall damage, provide an estimate to repair these damages.

Mold Bid Requirements

Measurements are required when submitting a bid to remove/clean mold or remediate any mold (in California all bids to remove/clean or remediate any mold should be supplied by a contractor who is licensed to do so.)

When bidding mold removal, make sure to include the following:
- A description of exactly what is being completed. Are you just cleaning, applying any type of antifungal chemical, removing, and/or replacing?
- The number of rooms affected and the area size. Submit several photos of the rooms affected and make sure the photos show the areas specified in your bid.
- Always bid to correct the cause of the mold.
- If mold is extensive and will require testing and a certified abatement contractor to remove the mold, indicate this on your update, providing a good description of the areas affected and an estimate of the damages.

If any of the above information is not included in your update, the order will be left open and you will be requested to supply the missing information. Photos are always required to support any work being bid or damages being reported.

Dehumidifiers
Install Dehumidifier to rectify moisture issues that may be causing or can cause mold damage to a property.

Freeze damage
This category includes broken pipes, frozen/broken toilets, or cracked heating systems as a result of freezing temperatures. Frozen toilets need a bid to thaw or remove and replace. If the whole house is frozen you need to submit bids to thaw; include the method of thawing, the materials used to thaw, the amount of time needed to thaw, and the cost per "man hour." For example, (3-propane heaters, 2-fans, 6 hours) always bid to pressure test once house is thawed to look for leaks. Freeze Damage can cause pipes to break or burst. In these cases, contractors should supply bids to repair pipes or bid plumbing contractor to evaluate system.

Sump Pumps

On all properties that a sump pump is present, follow work order instructions and update to have utilities turned on in client's name. On most REO initial work orders there is an allowable to replace inoperable sump pumps without providing a bid. Read the work order, if no allowable is mentioned call your company office from site to see if we can get over the phone approval to replace the sump pump while you are at the property. Provide a photo of the sump pump even if it's working. Take before, during, and after photos of any work completed including replacing the sump pump.

The sump pump must be checked in order to determine it is operable. If there is standing water in the basement, advise how deep the water is and submit a bid to pump the basement. Remember to submit all bids necessary in order to get the sump pump operable. If there is a hole for a sump pump yet no sump pump has ever been installed, provide all the bids necessary to put an operable sump pump in that hole. Contractors are required to submit a receipt for the purchase of a new sump pump, along with the necessary photos.

Swamp Coolers

Swamp coolers require the water supply to be shut off to the unit and the water in the base emptied and then covered to protect it from the elements when they are not in use.

Crime/Biohazards/Methamphetamine Labs

Should a contractor run across any items thought to represent criminal activity, biohazards, or a meth lab, get out of house and contact your company immediately?

METHAMPHETAMINE POSTING: If there is a posting that the property is a Methamphetamine, Chemical or "Clandestine" laboratory, contractors should NOT enter the property and should notify your company immediately.
These warnings are different than "Closed to Occupancy."

CORONER'S SEAL: If there is a coroner's seal on a property the contractor should not do work.

Posted Closed to Occupancy
The contractor should call the number on the "Closed to Occupancy" sign and inquire as to why the property was posted. Often it was due to the water being shut off and squatters were living inside. After inquiry call your company office with the explanation and to get further instruction.
As part of your due diligence, don't forget to look for other signs of Environmental Damage. Mold is in every home although most of it is not dangerous. Look for visible water damage, stained walls.
Don't touch it or tear anything out. Mold is a money maker and has to be removed properly. Order a mold test.

Look for burn marks on walls, bleach stained carpet, holes in walls, bluish discoloration on metal, missing fire extinguishers, burn piles in back yard, strange hooks on walls where hooks would normally not be seen or appearance of not caring as these are all signs of meth. Meth is a money maker and is more prevalent than you will ever know. Order a test.

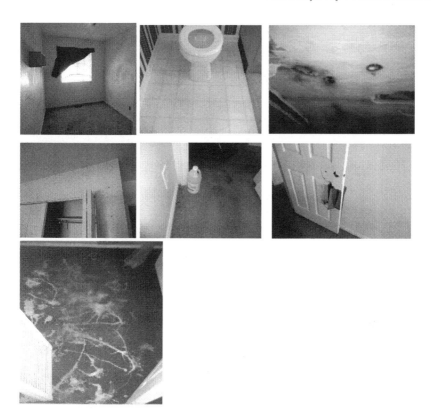

Additional Bids

Safety Issues -Missing Smoke Detectors/C02 Detectors.
Install all missing smoke detectors as per code at the time of the initial services are performed, supply before, during and after photos to support work.

Safety Issues -Exposed Electrical Wiring
Bid to cap all exposed electrical wires, provide photos to support bid.

Safety Issues -Exposed Electric Covers/Outlets
Bid to cover all exposed electrical covers and outlets, provide photos to support bid.

Safety Issues – Non-capped Gas Lines
Bid to cap all uncapped gas lines, provide photos to support bid.

Damages/Hazard Claims

Damage Procedures
One of the most common areas that require detailed reporting is property damage. Many of the estimates submitted are used by the mortgage company for filing of insurance claims for vandalism, storm or wind damages, theft or missing items, fire/smoke damage, flood or water damage, freeze damage, mortgagor neglect, or structural damages. You will always be required to provide an estimate of the amount of damage and the source of the damage such as "active roof leak in living room area."

Companies are required to provide a thorough update regarding the cause of any property damage we report. If all required information is not supplied on your initial update and we have to follow-up with you to obtain information, the filing of the insurance claim is delayed for at least that follow-up time. Such delays can ultimately have a negative effect on the client's recovery for the loss. Your cooperation in reporting property damage as discussed below will reduce the amount of time we spend tracking down important information and to timely address important property issues.

IMPORTANT: In all cases where a property has sustained damage, we need a date of loss (the date of the fire, water damage, flood, or vandalism occurred, if available) or a date of discovery of damage so that an insurance claim can be filed promptly.

If any insurance claimable damage is found (water, roof leak, fire, freeze, vandalism etc.) provide photo documentation and an estimate to support the claim. Make sure to include enough photo documentation to support the estimate so the insurance company and our customer can get a good view of the damage.

Updating Procedures for Hazard Claim Repairs

All repairs must be updated on a (minimum) weekly basis. An update form will be emailed to each repair contractor every Monday. This repair update must be either filled out or emailed or the update may be called in. Each repair update must be submitted by Tuesday morning. The update form includes: the anticipated completion date, a request for a list of completed repairs, as well as, a request for a list of repairs scheduled for the following week. Repeated failure to submit updates in a timely manner could negatively affect your status as a repair contractor.

If the weekly update form is not received, it is still the contractor's responsibility to update a repair analyst on the repair progress.

The contractor must notify your company as soon as he/she becomes aware that the originally scheduled completion date will not be met. The adjusted completion date will need to be forwarded to the client as soon as possible.

Written authorization is needed prior to beginning any additional repairs.

YOUR COMPANY must be updated immediately if there are any problems during the repair process such as:

- Any hidden damages discovered during the repair process. (Such as mold found behind sheetrock or meth contamination)
- Any new damages discovered (such as vandalism, broken windows, etc.)
- Any new violations or citations posted at the property. If an inspector cites new violations while repairing the property, please request that the violation be documented in writing.

Any additional repairs which are not per the original estimate or per the adjuster's scope must be bid and then forwarded to the client for approval. Contractors must receive written authorization from YOUR COMPANY in order to be compensated for additional repairs. Any additional repairs completed without prior authorization cannot be reimbursed.

Water Damage
Water damage as with all major damages your report must include a possible cause for the damages (e.g. broken pipe(s), roof leak, sump pump back-up, toilet overflow, etc.) and What is damaged (floor, ceiling, carpet, cabinets, etc.)? Be sure that you completely and accurately report all damage and photo document the extent of all the damage.

Flood Damage
Do not report flood damage if you meant water damage. It is critical that you properly evaluate damage to determine if it is attributable to actual flooding or to other sources of water damage, and that

you provide an accurate description of the damage and an analysis of its cause.

Vandalism

Most insurance carriers require a police report to be filed when vandalism is discovered.

Unfinished Renovations

The term "unfinished renovations" should only be used when it is certain that a building permit has been issued. It is difficult to determine if a property is being renovated or if items have been removed with no intent to put anything back. The term "missing item" or "items" should be used, i.e. missing sheetrock, missing toilet, cabinet, flooring, etc. Always provide quantities or sizes of items or area.

Property Repair Work Orders

Each repair work order must be reviewed carefully in order to determine the intent of repairs. Repairs are generally the result of work orders completed for an REO Initial Secure or for Hazard Insurance Claims. The end result of most repairs is to put the property into marketable condition; however, each repair work order must be carefully reviewed by the contractor in order to determine the intent of the repair.

Property Repairs

Additional repairs, beyond the approved scope of work, MUST be authorized by your company and our customer. Hazard claim repairs must be updated on a weekly basis.

Upon receipt of client authorization to begin property repairs, your company will issue a repair work order to the bidding contractor. A work order will be emailed to the contractor which includes all pertinent information needed for successful repair completion. All new repair work orders will include the following information: (See next page for sample report)

- Approved estimate sum -for which repairs are to be completed. Any additional repairs CANNOT be done without prior client authorization.
- Request for start and completion dates -dates must be called in by the contractor to your company within 2 days of receipt of the work order.
- Photo Information -photo policy and request for duplicate photos if the repair is the result of an insurance claim.
- Update Information -must be submitted (either called in or emailed) on a weekly basis.
- If the repairs are to be completed per the insurance scope a copy of the adjuster's estimate will be sent with the order. The adjuster's scope is only for the insurance claimable damage and not all the damage in a house. THE REPAIRS MUST BE DONE PER THE ADJUSTER'S ESTIMATE AND SCOPE TO REVCEIVE FULL PAYMENT FOR THE ORDER.

Repair Photo Policy
Before, during, and after photos MUST be documented for all repairs.
Photos are an important part of the repair process. Photos should be taken on a daily basis during repairs, not just once at the end of repairs (especially in high crime areas). The following guidelines should be followed for repair photos:

- Before, during and after photos are required for all repair orders to ensure proper documentation of the work being performed.
- The "before" photo of the item repaired is to be followed by the "during" and "after" photos of the repair. The before and after photos must be taken from the same angle and clearly show the work that was completed.
- Photos are to be submitted as quickly as possible after repair completion.
- If the repair photos do not adequately justify the work authorized, the contractor may be required to take additional photos before final payment is issued.

CHAPTER 7

Control Your Labor-Control Your Life

Controlling Labor Production Pay/Piece Rate

Let me tell you an all too common story. The early 2000's were a dream come true for home owners, business owners, business executives as it seemed like anything we produced, it sold. Any business that was going well prior to 2000, improved by leaps and bounds. Credit was easy to establish. Buy now, pay later! Purchase a second, third home with equity from another home. Consumers were excited to spend. Investors were coming out of the woods and everything was working so well. It just felt the sky was the limit.

I was introduced to an owner of a large HVAC company. This particular company sold air condition and heating units to residential homes. They also maintained the units. The owner let me know that they were installing an average of 45 units per week for over 10 years in a row. In two particular years, the company averaged over 60 units per week. The company invested heavily in equipment, training and tools to manage this company. The company owned 17 vans for installation and repair. The teams were working 40-50 hours per week and the company was making a lot of revenue and the profits were good enough to put away $50-60,000 per month in the business operations fund. The crews were like family to this owner and he simply didn't mind paying overtime because the profits were good. The owner felt as if he had achieved his dreams and couldn't imagine the business doing anything but well.

The business started to change back in 2008 when the economy started to change. This business owner felt as if he could probably withstand a slight drop in the economy as he had a large operations fund ($1.2 million) and didn't imagine this dip in business to last more than a season or two. He felt that he had such a great team and together they would all pull through this downturn.

It's now 2012 and the business is currently in bankruptcy and his largest creditor is selling off vehicles, equipment and the inventory. Gone is the $1.2 million in operations capital, the large line of credit and the owner is back in a van repairing equipment. The owner did not go out of business but he did step back 20 years and has very little to show for it. He is currently 57 years of age. He doesn't anticipate being able to retire for another 20 years.

The following information will help you and your business avoid the same type of tragedy. Hopefully you will be inspired and see the warning signs.

Why Did You Go Into Business?

One of the first questions I ask to every business owner was why they chose their profession and what is their expectation? Many people are not meant to be business owners and many are not called to be employees. How did we get here? Now that you are here, what is your expectation and do you have a strong enough "why" to get you to get off your duff? Did you go in business to pay others or did you go into business for yourself?

Buying Your Clients

Too many business owners don't understand the cost of going into business. I would rather buy an existing business and make it better instead of buying a new business. The biggest reason why so many businesses fail is they don't understand acquisition costs of new clients. Acquisition cost is what it cost you to get a new client. **Example:** If you spent $2,000 on a marketing piece and you received 20 new clients out of this piece, your acquisition cost is now $100 per customer. That is wonderful if your service or product is a high ticket item or your product/service is something that is ongoing. It is not so good for the owner if your product/service is a one-time purchase and the purchase was less than the acquisition cost.

I mentioned that that the biggest reason why so many businesses fail is they don't understand acquisition costs. If you do the math and your acquisition cost is $25 per client and your business needs 1,000 clients to hit your break even mark, your marketing costs will need to exceed $25,000. When most small businesses start up, they normally don't budget $25,000 for marketing and then they wonder why they fail.

One of the key elements of creating a great business is figuring out how to lower your acquisition cost and increase the lifetime value of your clients. The only way you can lower your acquisition cost is by measuring everything and getting better. Try out new marketing pieces and measures which ones give the most bang for your buck.

Save Your Business

The information so far has been simply to set the tone:

- Nobody cares about your business as much as you.
- Employees waste 30% of your time and money doing unproductive items.
- When your business has a downturn, you'll find that your staff simply wants to be paid and doesn't care if you are paid.
- You went into business for yourself, not everyone else.
- You must understand what a customer is worth to your business.
- Labor is your number one cost.

Saving your business comes down to two items: 1. Continuous marketing 2. Controlling all of your costs. Being that labor is your number one cost, the rest of this information booklet has to do with the nuts and bolts of where you can control labor and how to do it.

Chapter 8

Introduction to Piece Rate

What's the incentive for your staff on hourly rate? None! Individual incentive plans offer the clearest link between a worker's effort and the reward. Probably the best known individual or small group incentive pay plan is *piece rate*. Piece rate had been more suited to repetitive crew work (e.g., housekeeping, lawn cuts, etc) than to office work. As the tie between individual work and results is diminished, so is the motivating effect of the incentive on the individual.

My background is growing business, controlling costs and helping individuals across the country realize the dream of owning a business. Most of my education comes from my college background and years of testing and measuring. I have built businesses and have used these techniques to become more profitable. According to Randall Bartlett at Smith College, there are six principles of human behavior accepted by economists for making decisions:

1. People Respond to Incentives
2. No Free Lunch Due to Scarcity
3. Must Know the Opportunity Cost of Any Decision
4. All Actions Have Unintended Consequences
5. One Never Can do Just One Thing
6. Nobody Is Truly in Control

The objective of this introduction is to summarize much of this work, and give clear and precise suggestions for the effective design of piece rate pay and controlling your labor costs. A number of serious challenges that threaten the effectiveness of this pay method are also included. While my work has been primarily in cleaning and handyman, the principles can be easily adapted to other types of work.

Gregorio Billikoff wrote on his thesis; I was taken aback by the assertion of a colleague at the University of California, Davis, "Civilized nations," he argued, "have moved away from paying by the piece." Certainly, there are articles and papers on the death of piece rate. While piece rate is still utilized widely, it often fails to motivate employees as much as it could. Greed—on both sides— often gets in the way. Traditionally both the employer and worker have come to believe that the other is out to cheat him. Piece rate, rightfully so, is often associated with a game played between the two.

Employers can build piece rate systems that prevent workers from earning higher wages at the expense of the enterprise. But just as important, employers can (and should) design piece rate approaches that help build worker motivation and trust. What is at stake is a sustainable pay system with the potential to greatly benefit both employer and employee in the long run. Owners can reduce costs while increasing productivity. Workers can earn substantially greater amounts. Such enterprises are likely to have a waiting list of excellent people who wish to work for them and have little to worry when talk of labor shortages are raised.

When we're dealing with employees, framing and reframing are important aspects of negotiation—of viewing issues from a particular perspective. I always ask my employees, "How would you feel if some of your crew workers made twice the minimum wage and you still made money? Without fail the answer is that this would be great. "How about three times the minimum wage?" I inquired next. "Would that make you nervous?"

The fact of the matter is that your staff can and will make a lot more if and when Piece Rate is implemented properly. Certainly, the very thought of your staff earning three or more times the minimum wage would send some business owners straight to the trauma center. The owners are likely to feel that they made a mistake when they set up their piece rate. One need to reframe, then, has to do with the bottom line. Instead of panicking at the hourly equivalent that a piece-rate paid worker is earning, look at the bottom line such as cost per lawn, cost per house cleaned, cost per loaf, cost per square ft., etc.

Put another way, in the form of a question: "Does your company make more money as your staff makes more money?" If the answer is a 'maybe' or a 'no,' your pay for performance design is faulty. If the answer is a 'yes,' why worry because some of your staff is going home with their pockets full of money?

I spoke earlier about framing and reframing are aspects of negotiation. They are also aspects of trust. Once your staff starts making a good living, some of your staff will be nervous that you will cut their piece-rate pay—either now or next year—if they perform at their full potential. Some owners who have understood and overcome this trust issue have had employees make three times the minimum wage and more.

As the business owners must:

1. Find the right piece rate percentage.
2. Communicate it to the staff.

3. Find the staff enough work to make a decent living.
4. Bid properly.
5. Don't change the percentage. Also, don't start the piece rate too high. Once you start it too high, you can't go back easily. Without a doubt, nothing can kill worker motivation faster than having the piece rate lowered—or the fear of the same.

Starting the process of piece rate requires a degree of boldness especially for those that were paid hourly wages from the commencement of your business. Be prepared to lose staff because it will happen. Everyone "knows" someone that was on piece rate of production pay that was "cheated" out of pay. Some simply won't give it a chance and will leave immediately. Some will start the process and won't see the vision of the earning potential or don't understand the value of additional time and will leave. For those that stick it out, confidence and trust will build over time for both sides.

Once you make the commitment, stay with it! The price for being consistent will pay off for your staff and your business!

Where Can I Control My Labor?

The simple answer to that question is <u>everywhere.</u> The fact of the matter is that all jobs including office staff can be controlled:

- Property Preservation
- Housekeeping – Percentage of the job
- Handyman – Percentage of the job
- Yard Care – Percentage of the job
- Supervisor/Manager for any department. Small salary plus incentives to grow their departments.

- Subcontractors – Percentage of the job.
- Office Staff – Set the hours.
- Elder Care – Elder Care is normally paid by the hour so you simply pay your staff by the same amount of hours that you bill. The job starts and ends on the site of the patient.
- Medical Care – Paid by the patient
- Sales – Small salary plus commission for short period of time until small salary is taken away.

How Do I Control My Labor?

Controlling labor is quite simple but we as business owners like to make it too difficult. There is always a reason, "why it won't work." The fact of the matter is that it does work in 95% of all situations. The only time it doesn't work at is when all of your work orders are spread hours apart. In that case, the business owner must bid for the travel time or find part time workers/contractors to do each job individually in the different areas and paid a percentage of the job.

Piece rate stems from the premises that your workers are only guaranteed minimum wage for their time. Let me repeat that part. All employees are minimum wage employees and must sign a document stating such. All employees must keep track of their time. Dollars earned at the end of the week must be divided into the hours worked. If your staff does not earn enough in the week to be paid minimum wage, you must pay them the difference. Piece rate is also a great filter. If your staff only earns minimum wage, you don't want them but they usually quit first after they get their first check.

For Building Contractor services, it is always best to hire subcontractors. The reasons for it is they use their own equipment, have their own insurance, tools and you as the owner ALWAYS make a profit on every job. Subcontractors need to be treated as if they own their own businesses. Put the majority of the responsibility on the subcontractor for bidding, taking pictures, doing the work and the majority of the uploading. If you allow your subcontractors to do a bad job from the beginning, they will always cause you anguish. Be sure to find someone you know, like and trust from the beginning. If the subcontractor fails to improve, simply don't send them any more work. Position your subcontractors that they will receive work as long as they do good work, find additional work and get it back to you on time. If any of the three don't occur, you will not send them any work. Your name is on the work order, not your subcontractor!

As the business owner, your main responsibility is to find work and to train. Be sure to adequately train your subcontractors using your own manuals and be sure to have contracts and agreements in place.

For most services that you perform, it is better to simply give your subcontractor a price sheet for the services they will be performing. They make money off of volume and finding additional work. Typically contractors are not great at finding work so they simply get work by doing good work for your business. Contractors must guarantee their work.

Bidding additional work takes some coordination between yourself and your subcontractor. Your subcontractor does not submit the bid to the client; that is your responsibility. Make sure you mark up any additional work so that it takes into account all your overhead fees. **Example:** Your subcontractor bids an additional $1000 to remove limbs that are touching a house, replaces two cracked windows and removes dirt from the window wells. Your subcontractor may be of the thought that he/she will be keeping all the additional $1,000 because that may be his/her costs to do the work. In that case, we need to add your overhead and profit on top of it. You still pay your subcontractor the set percentage of the job

For **Housekeeping, Yard, Handyman.** Each of these types of jobs is to be paid a percentage of the job. **Example:** If you bid $150 for any type of job, you should pay no more than 35% for the job. At 35%, you would pay your staff $52.50. If there is more than one person, they split the $52.50. Don't pay more for any reason!

Percentages: Remember that your staff and your business are only as good as your bid. You want to pay your staff a great wage. If you are the lowest guy in town, you won't be able to pay a good wage and your staff will leave you. Educate your customer and give them value. You absolutely cannot be the lowest bidder in town. If you live by price, you will die by price! Stay away from price strategies and concentrate on education and value added services.

The following is a list of labor percentages for the different types of jobs:

	Excellent	**Marginal**	**Poor**
Cleaning	Less than 26%	27-35%	Over 35%
Handyman	Less than 28%	29-35%	Over 35%
Yard	Less than 26%	27-35%	Over 35%
MFS	Less than 26%	27-35%	Over 35%

Administrative: Many times administrative costs can go through the roof. Many companies bring someone on from the inception of the business. If this is the case for your company, make sure that the administrative person allows you to Market and Train your staff. If you find that you are spending too much time doing administrative items, you have the wrong person. You want to get to a place where your administrative labor is 6% or less of your total revenue. Your administrative person needs to know that they will be required to do everything in the office from answering telephones, ordering supplies, cleaning, assigning work orders, taking payment, finances, motivating, marketing, following up, etc. If you hire an administrative person from the inception, they must be thought of as an investment so that you can get out to market and train. Your 6% ratio needs to come into line within 6 months or you should cut the hours. Another way to control your administrative person is simply allow that person to work based on revenue. **Example:** If you have scheduled $5,000 in business that week, divide the $5,000 by 6% = $300. If you pay your administrative person $11 per hour, he/she will have 27 1/4 hours ($11 x 27.25 hrs. = $299.75) of available time to work that week. The right person will be motivated to help find more work and motivate the owners to get out there so that you can increase the admin hours. Many companies will use the same guide but pay the hours the following week as many times it is difficult to determine how much revenue is scheduled before the week starts.

Your administrative people are there to make things run better and for you to look better. I use the example of John Stockton of the Utah Jazz. He made everyone around him a better basketball player. He gave excellence and demanded excellence from everyone. When players left the Utah Jazz, they never (without fail) were as successful. If your administrative persons don't make you a better owner and your staff better, you have the wrong person.

Supervisors are similar to administrative people. Supervisors are not "divas" or "bosses" in the sense that when you start a business, they must be working supervisors. Supervisors should not be retained until the owner is in a place where bidding and working interfere with each other. Hire a Supervisor after the bidding ration takes up half their work time per week. The reason is because that is the point where the owner is earning enough that it doesn't make sense for the owner to be actually working on the job because his/her hourly rate is to a point that bidding brings in 4 to 5 times more in revenue than one would be paid to do the work. If an owner is bringing in more than $55 an hour for finding work, why would the owner ever do work that he/she could pay someone $10-15 an hour to perform?

Supervisors are under the same scrutiny as normal staff. They are still paid piece rate for the jobs they are doing and should not be made Supervisors until there is more than 40 hours a week of work. While the business is still in its infancy, the owners may be required to have staff doing some of the bidding. The problem that could occur is that under the "piece rate" system, your staff does not get paid to do bids because bidding is not a paid job. For this reason, it sometimes becomes necessary to give an allowable payment to your Supervisors so that they can find work. **Example:** While growing any department, it would make sense to pay a weekly "salary" of $320. This will guarantee a full time Supervisor earns a minimum of $8 an hour for a 40 hour work week. If the Supervisor earns more than $320 from piece rate while working, we pay the Supervisor the greater amount. (Set $320 or money earned from working) During the Supervisor's slow time each day, they may be doing bids, passing out flyers, marketing, following up on leads, etc.

You must have set expectations as well. When passing out flyers, it is expected that they track where they deliver and hand out a minimum of 85 flyers per hour. There becomes a point with the Supervisor that you they will be doing more administrative, training, following up on leads, hiring, discipline and bidding that pull the Supervisors away from doing actual work. In those cases, it is best to set up fees for each of their activities.

The following is simply an example of how to track and pay a Supervisor

YARD SUPERVISOR

Supervisor Jobs		Rate	Number Per Week	Weekly Total
Base Rate				320
Odd Jobs Assigned by Owner		15	2	30
Wash Vehicles		10	5	50
Inspecting Jobs		15	7	105
Clean Shop Once a Week		15	1	15
Train Staff Meetings		15	5	75
Bids Won		15	4	60
	Total			$ 655.00
Employee Name:	Steffan Ray			
Week Ending:	14-Dec-11			
Please hand in the Admin on Monday after:				14-Dec-11
Vehicles must be washed by Supervisor				
Vehicle must be cleaned by Superviosr				
All Inspection sheets turned in daily				

The Supervisor should always receive the greater amount from the work or salary but would be incentivized to do the other aspects of their job. The above-mentioned are simply recommendations. Your Supervisors are working Supervisors and are not to be in the office for very much time. The only reasons for your Supervisors to be in the office more than a half hour per day is because you are training them, they are training a staff member or they are creating a bid or marketing piece. Keep track of your Supervisor's time and do not allow them to get comfortable for any reason. It's ok if your Supervisor earns over $50k annually. That means they helped bring in four to five times more in their department.

Paying Mileage: As a rule of thumb, do not pay mileage. On occasion, staff members use their own vehicles. It is not recommended because they might not have the proper insurance and if they wreck into another car or do personal damage, your insurance many not cover them and you may be headed into a lawsuit. If someone used their vehicle for work, it is better to pay them a gas stipend rather than mileage. **Example:** pay someone $50 per week if they use their equipment as an employee. Don't pay contractors any sort of mileage. I saw one business owner pay .40 cents per mile. The employee drove nearly 200 miles per day and the employer ended up paying hundreds of dollars per week. In one case, the owner was paying out nearly $1,000 per week. It would have been less expensive to buy three new vehicles and pay for all fill ups, repairs and oil changes. Don't get caught in this trap because your profit will go straight down the drain.

Payroll:

One of the questions that arise is: How do I keep the labor board out of my office? That is a great question and will come up from your staff without fail. Most of your staff has not worked under piece rate and may feel that we are "ripping them off". It is an easy fix.

All staff members **MUST** track their hours. We don't pay overtime. Everyone is hired as a minimum wage employee. Rather than pay overtime, hire an additional staff member that starts early in the afternoon. Overtime will kill your margins. Everyone tracks their labor. At the end of each week, you simply divide all "piece rate" dollars earned by their amount of hours worked. **Example:** Your handyman earns $600 and works 30 hours during that week. The time includes their travel time. This means your handyman earned $20 per hour. ($600 divided by 30 hours = $20 per hour) As the employer, you must 1) track dollars earned and average hourly rate for the week and 2) a running total for the year. If the labor board shows up, you simply showed them that they earned more than minimum wage. In most every single case, your staff will be earning more than the local average hourly rate. As you learn to bid, your staff will earn more than the average hourly rate.

Made in the USA
Lexington, KY
23 April 2015